MOVEMENT EDUCATION LEADING TO

GYMNASTICS 4-7:

A SESSION-BY-SESSION APPROACH TO KEY STAGE 1

ACKNOWLEDGEMENTS

Photographs: Les Cross, Brighton Polytechnic

Children from Bevendean Primary School, Brighton

Illustrations: Marilyn Amos

MOVEMENT EDUCATION LEADING TO GYMNASTICS 4-7: A SESSION-BY-SESSION APPROACH TO KEY STAGE 1

H.K. MANNERS

and

M.E. CARROLL
Brighton Polytechnic

(A member of the Taylor & Francis Group)
LONDON, NEW YORK & PHILADELPHIA

UK The Falmer Press, 4 John St, London WC1N 2ET
USA The Falmer Press, Taylor & Francis Inc., 1990 Frost Road, Suite 101, Bristol, PA 19007

First published in 1991
Reprinted 1993, 1994

British Library Cataloging in Publication Data
A catalogue record for this book is ISBN 0 75070 007 6 is available from the British Library.

Book and cover design by Caroline Archer

Typesetting by Blackmore Typesetting Services

CONTENTS

PREFACE

This teachers' workbook is a newly designed Key Stage 1 (Infant years R - 2) version of the original **Gymnastics 7-11** by M E Carroll and D Garner first published in 1984 and reprinted several times since. It is the first of a two-volume workbook; the second being a completely revised version of the 1984 edition entitled **Gymnastics 7-11: A Session-by-Session Approach to Key Stage 2** by M E Carroll and H K Manners.

The need for this volume became self-evident once **Gymnastics 7-11** was published. Teachers of the younger child asked for the same kind of session-by-session approach which would meet their own particular needs, and which would be in line with likely developments in respect of the National Curriculum.

Both volumes follow a similar format and approach and are designed to be a progressively developing programme of work from Year R – Year 6 ie: Key Stages 1 and 2.

ME Carroll
HK Manners
Brighton Polytechnic
April 1991

INTRODUCTION

Children learn by doing. A baby lying on a carpet will quickly learn to roll over from his back to his tummy and vice versa. Once mobile he uses movement to explore his environment, often climbing onto obstacles before he can walk. He responds to verbal instructions in a physical way, learning to understand phrases like, 'come over here', 'sit down', 'put your coat on' and so on. Playing with his toys he improves manipulative skills and on his tricycle he learns to push the pedals with his feet, to steer and swerve by shifting his weight, to stop by pulling on the brakes.

Whilst climbing, walking and running he is struggling to master balance and co-ordination, increasing his strength and, for example, seeing how high he dare go, he tests and challenges himself, all the time learning what his body can and cannot do.

These natural actions of rolling, climbing, running, jumping and sliding combined with controlling the weight of the body whilst moving, form the basis of Movement Education which in turn leads to Gymnastics, and the purpose of this book is to help teachers to provide a 'Gymnastics' environment' in which children can progress at their own rate from moving instinctively and hesitantly to performing competently, with understanding and awareness.

What is involved in Gymnastics

Definitions are often difficult and imprecise. A definition of Gymnastics is not necessarily helpful – yet it is necessary to know what characterizes the work. It would seem that whatever form of Gymnastics is evident (Olympics, rhythmic, educational, sports acrobatics, vaulting and agility) certain kinds of attributes give the work its name Gymnastics. It has several components worth examining; although these may seem irrelevant up to **Key Stage 1**, it is helpful to see where the infant work is leading.

Physical component
This includes:
(i) A degree of strength sufficient for the work to be performed safely.
(ii) A degree of flexibility sufficient to enable the safe execution of many aspects – mainly shoulder, hip, ankle flexibility.

Skill component (with or without apparatus)
This includes running, jumping and landing, balance, and rotation.

Aesthetic component
A concern
(i) for the shape and line of the action where the child concentrates on the beauty of his movements;
(ii) for the kinaesthetic satisfaction of having got it just right.

Creative component
True creativity shown by some international gymnasts is reflected in novel movements derived from a structured and disciplined training. At a lower level, however, the child can be seen to produce/create movements and a series of movements which may be novel to himself.

Psychological component
This includes:
(i) A degree of courage.
(ii) A degree of perseverance.

Cognitive component
An understanding of how the body moves.

If then these factors need to be present for the activity to be called Gymnastics, and if the work is to happen in school, then a teaching approach throughout must be adopted which will, on the one hand, generate the development of these essential characteristics and, on the other, will also be a relevant educational experience. Children should therefore be able to demonstrate bodily skill on the floor, on apparatus, and at times with a partner, because this is the aim of the work.

How a teacher achieves such an aim is the next stage of the argument.

It is here that the differing needs of the developing child must be considered. The young infant (in school) is using the 'Gymnastic' environment to explore a range of movement options – and as already stated this exploration may be clumsy and unrefined. The role of the teacher at this stage is to intervene to make the children *conscious* of what they are doing, so that they are both *moving* and *knowing*.

As the children become mature, in the later primary years **(Key Stage 2)**, the teacher seeks to develop more stylized, skilled bodily action-which has a clearer resemblance to recognized gymnastic forms. By the end of the later primary years, children should be capable of demonstrating skilled and harmonious body action, showing discrimination in their selection of work to practise and perform.

So within these phases of development:
If Gymnastics is about bodily skill (as it undoubtedly is), and if we want our children to be proficient in using skilled bodily movement in answer to various kinds of tasks, the method adopted must operate fully along the methodological continuum of open-ended (process) – closed (product). It makes sense to do this since some activities require direct teaching, whereas others, particularly in the early years, lend themselves to a more experimental approach. Sometimes the teacher will set tasks which tightly constrain what the children may do (*eg.* run and stop). At other times, children may need to demonstrate understanding of a movement concept in their performance and so the task will be of a different order (*eg.* find a way of travelling with your feet together). There are also many other stages in between which are more or less constraining.

In both volumes of these workbooks these stages feature in a structured, progressive form. Different kinds of tasks are given which demand different kinds of response from the children. The whole two volume programme has an inbuilt development of skill learning, movement understanding and composing.

The Approach

In order to facilitate the ordering of subject matter, and its presentation to children, the whole programme is written in session format. The sessions are planned so that they develop the material of Gymnastics in different forms, in order to ensure progression of skill, of movement understanding and of individual response to movement tasks. How these sessions are used will vary according to facilities, apparatus, the ability of the children, the expertise of the teacher and the time available. Each session can be treated as a lesson in itself, or spread over several lessons. IN FACT SOME SESSIONS WILL NEED TO BE REPEATED. The session can be adapted, developed, or used for consolidation.

There are ten sessions for each of the autumn and spring terms, making way in the summer for outdoor games, swimming and sports activities. However there is no reason why the sessions should not be extended into the summer term if preferred.
Each session is divided into four sections. The warming up activities are designed to familiarize the children with the hall space, getting them to focus their attention on the teacher and also provide some vigorous activity to increase the heart rate.

In the second section the children explore a range of ideas on the floor which can then be transferred and adapted onto the apparatus in the third section. This gives the children the challenge of moving on wide and narrow surfaces, sloping situations, climbing high on the frame and swinging on the ropes etc. The last section is designed to calm the children down before returning to the classroom.

The Content
Session format is as follows:

Content	**Teaching Points**
The task which is given to the children	The emphases needed for ensuring satisfactory response to the work and/or notes to the teacher.

The content of the sessions varies in three ways:

1 Simple activities we do all together, (including the teacher) developing a corporate sense of belonging.

2 Challenges in which the children, through exploration, try to find their own ways of responding, working individually and discovering their own capabilities.

3 Ideas are put forward to help children create patterns of movements which can be repeated and performed, thus aiding their sequential skills and movement memories. With Reception these can be referred to as movement 'stories' but there is no reason why they can not be referred to as movement phrases with the older children.

In the Reception class, language plays an important part, and emphasis is put on naming the actions children choose to do, introducing them to some of the terminology and identifying parts of the body involved in the movement.

In Year 1, this conscious awareness of what the children are doing is exploited to increase their understanding and skill, together with learning about how the space around them can be used to good advantage. Situations in which the children learn to use this knowledge, together with more control and skill, is put to greater use in Year 2 during which the movements begin to be more Gymnastic-like in nature.

At the end of each term there is an assessment and consolidation session which indicates what it is hoped the children will have learnt. The session can be used to make good any noted weaknesses and repeat any activity which the children found particularly enjoyable.

Notes about the use of apparatus are found at the start of each term's sessions.

Specific Skills Guide
Where tasks relate to teaching specific skills, reference should be made to the **Specific Skills Guide** at the end of the book. For information on teaching further skills see the second volume *A Session-by-Session Approach to Key Stage 2*. It is most important that this whole programme of Gymnastics from 4 - 11 is seen as a progressive learning package. Whilst it is recognized that when first introducing it into a school it may be necessary for older children to begin at the earlier stages if their experience is limited, in time there will only be a structured development of Gymnastics throughout the school if everyone works with the plan. *It is only when a school decides to use such a plan, AND works with it over a number of years, that real progress through Key Stages 1 and 2 will be seen in teaching of Gymnastics.*

Observation

As Physical Education is transient in nature it is difficult to observe and assess the responses of the children to the tasks, however this is a very necessary exercise since the way the children react will affect and influence what the teacher asks them to do next.

Children can also learn to observe each other's movements and this will help their understanding, assist their language development and increase the range of activities they can do.

It is possible to examine movement as follows:

Asking:

(i) WHAT? Actions are being done (Jumping, Running, Sliding etc)
Body parts are being used (Hands, Feet, Knees etc)
Body shape is being adopted (Tucked , long, spread)

(ii)	HOW?	Fast or slow: strongly or lightly
(iii)	WHERE?	On the spot Levels: high or low Directions: (forward, backwards, sideways, upwards etc.) Pathways: (curved, zig-zagged, straight)
(iv)	WITH WHOM?	Alone A partner

Apparatus

This workbook ideally requires the following apparatus for a class of 30; this ensures maximum activity. However, the programme can still be followed with less apparatus. Hoops supported on activity skittles, stage blocks (providing there are no splinters or staples in them) and even carpet tiles with non-slip backing can be used as stepping stones with the younger children. Soft play equipment, (foam blocks covered in vinyl are ideal to provide situations for the children to climb on, crawl through, slide down etc.):

- 4 Benches
- 8 mats 6' x 4' or 3' x 4'
- 4 8' planks
- 3 stools/stacking tables
- 1 bar box
- 1 climbing frame
- 1 agility/movement table.

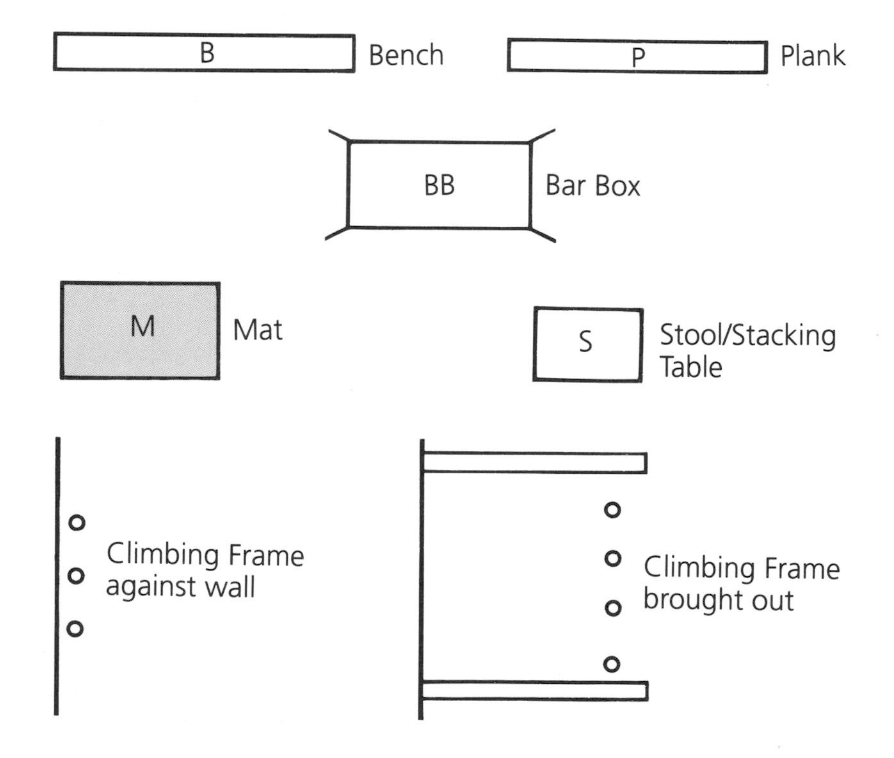

Safety

The safety of the children must be uppermost in the teacher's mind at all times, and in accordance with Local Authority regulations. A general agreed policy throughout the school will ensure safe and simple guidelines for every class teacher.

(i) The Hall

This area in most infant schools is a multi-use space and the following points need to be considered:-

(a) The floor should be clean, splinter-proof and non-slippery.
(b) The working area needs to be clear of displays, book shelves, pianos, overhead projectors etc. which provide dangerous corners if a child accidentally bumps into them.
(c) If used as a corridor, leave sufficient space for a direct route so that the classes are not disturbed.

(ii) Clothing

(a) Pupils should change into appropriate clothing for Gymnastic lessons, *i.e.* shorts or pants and tee shirt or vest. Sliding is an activity much enjoyed by children so some sort of top is desirable.
(b) Where the floor is suitable the children should work with bare feet.
(c) Jewellery should not be worn and long hair tied back.
(d) The teacher should also, of course, wear suitable clothing and safe footwear.

(iii) The Apparatus

(i) *General Comments*

(a) It is the responsibility of the teacher to make sure that any children handling apparatus do so correctly and safely.
(b) If apparatus is set out prior to the lesson, the teacher should check to see it is all secure before the children use it.
(c) Apparatus should be of a suitable height for the children. **Children should not** jump down from a height higher than themselves.
(d) Mats should be placed for children to land on after jumping from a piece of apparatus.

(ii) *Organization*

There are various ways of organizing the putting out of apparatus, depending on the age of the children and the apparatus available.

(a) The apparatus can be set out by adults beforehand – especially in the case of very young children and particularly if the apparatus is not really suitable for the children to handle (*ie.* is too heavy).
(b) Some apparatus can be put out beforehand and the rest placed at strategic positions around the sides of the room in readiness, so that all the children have to do is lift it into position. It saves time if the same children do the same job

each lesson *eg*. Mary and Tom lift the plank and hook it onto the bar box.

(c) The children can be taught to lift certain pieces of apparatus into position doing the same job each lesson, even though they may not necessarily work on that piece.

d) The children can be taught to handle all the apparatus, providing it is not too heavy, there is sufficient time to do this safely, and it is easily accessible.

(iii) *Handling Apparatus*

(a) There should be four children to each heavy piece – one at each side, they should lift it correctly, walk forwards whenever possible and place it down slowly and carefully.

(b) There should be four children to each mat, one at each corner. Mats should be lifted and not dragged and put away tidily.

(c) Planks must have a child at each end when they are being carried.

(d) **Nothing** should be carried over the heads of other children.

(e) All hooks, bolts etc. must be securely in position.

(iv) *Rules on the Apparatus*

(a) **No one** gets onto a piece of apparatus until told.

(b) The children must work quietly.

(c) Only one child on one piece of apparatus at a time, except the climbing frame.

(d) There should be no touching, helping or pushing other children.

(e) Children should get off the apparatus when told to do so and sit on the floor.

(f) **No** games are allowed to be played on apparatus.

Prefixing the session plans for each year and in Year 1 each term, there are notes on organization of the apparatus relative to the age group, re-enforcing what is written above.

The teacher must be positioned at all times where she can see the whole class.

The place of skill in the Early Years

Early Years children are flexible, agile and inquisitive. Through Gymnastics we want to channel these so that they become skilful in managing their bodies in a variety of situations. Thus the emphasis is on skilful control of the actions the child has chosen to do, rather than mastery of Gymnastic skills chosen by the teacher (although in order to extend the children there are one or two skills such as forward rolls deliberately included in the later sessions). Some specific skills are taught systematically in the second volume.

A teacher may have in her class a child who has been taught Gymnastic skills at a Club. The child can be very skilful at performing these specific skills and the teacher may be apprehensive about safety factors or worried that other children may try to emulate him. Much of the content of the sessions outlined here calls for individual, inventive responses very different from the way Gymnastics' clubs operate.

The teacher may need to explain this to the child and will certainly have to encourage him to be more inventive and try other ways of doing things. Discretion should be used when choosing such a child for demonstration purposes.

In particular, children tend to copy the movements of one who goes to a Gymnastics' Club when they are lacking in a range of ideas of their own to select from. Therefore the teacher needs to broaden their movement vocabulary by making suggestions and selecting a variety of examples for the class to watch and copy, keeping these examples within the ability range of the children so there is no risk of accidents.

The place of Demonstration

Children learn from doing, from each other, and from the teacher. Included in the session plans are opportunities for children to show what they have been doing. Demonstrations by individual children need to be purposeful. Half the class watching the rest can prove to be a non-productive use of precious time as those watching are unable to benefit from seeing so much going on at once.

The teacher can select a child to show the rest what to do in the event of a specific task about to be attempted, *eg.* a bunny hop. She may select a child to show the others how he has responded to a task, demonstrating originality, so they can then try out what he has done for themselves. Other children can be chosen to show good quality work (*eg.* good extension of the fingers and toes in a jump), or a child can be asked to show what he has done because, for him, it has been a real achievement.

In all instances it is best to confirm with the child first that he is prepared to demonstrate, and all demonstrations should be followed up by discussion with the children on what they have seen.

The teacher can demonstrate a movement to the children, *eg,* 'Can you do a star jump like this?' Or she can show the children how to start a movement off, *eg.* ' Put your hands on the floor like this and then try a crouch jump'. Whilst the children are working on the apparatus she might, for example, show a child where to put his hands in order to achieve a movement more successfully.

The main emphasis throughout all sessions should be on involvement on the part of the children, they need to have opportunity to use their boundless energy in a constructive, enjoyable way, resulting in a sense of achievement.

THE SESSION-BY-SESSION APPROACH TO KEY STAGE 1

KEY STAGE 1: OVERALL PLAN

RECEPTION

Autumn Term

Unit 1 Naming the actions

Session 1: Sit, stand, walk, run.
Session 2: Slide, spin, push, pull.
Session 3: Jumping and landing.
Session 4: Hopping and skipping.
Session 5: Rocking and rolling.

Unit 2 Familiarization with the space

Session 6: Finding a space.
Session 7: Moving to a new space.
Session 8: Stopping in a space.
Session 9: Big spaces.
Session 10: Small spaces

YEAR 1

Autumn Term

Unit 1 Being aware of the actions

Session 1: Going and stopping.
Session 2: Slide, spin, push, pull.
Session 3: Jumping and landing.
Session 4: Hopping and skipping.
Session 5: Rocking and rolling.

Unit 2 Being aware of the space

Session 6: Moving in and out of each other.
Session 7: Big and small
Session 8: High and low.
Session 9: Up to and away from.
Session 10: Wide and narrow.

YEAR 2

Autumn Term

Unit 1 Using the actions.

Session 1: Walk, run and stop.
Session 2: Slide, spin, push, pull.
Session 3: Jumping, hopping and skipping.
Session 4: With rotation (turning).
Session 5: To travel quickly or slowly.
Session 6: To travel strongly or lightly.

Unit 2 Using the space

Session 7: Going in different directions.
Session 8: Going forwards and backwards.
Session 9: Going up and down.
Session 10: Going sideways.

RECEPTION

Spring Term

Unit 3 Identifying parts of the body

Session 1: Feet and hands.
Session 2: Feet and hands (2).
Session 3: Arms and legs.
Session 4: Arms and legs (2).
Session 5: Backs, tummies and heads.
Session 6: Knees and elbows.

Unit 4 Positional language

Session 7: On and off.
Session 8: Under and over.
Session 9: In and out.
Session 10: Along and across.

YEAR 1

Spring Term

Unit 3 Being aware of parts of the body

Session 1: Touching the floor with hands and feet.
Session 2: Touching the floor with different parts.
Session 3: Travelling on hands and feet.
Session 4: Travelling on hands and feet (2).
Session 5: Travelling on backs, tummies, knees and elbows.

Unit 4 Holding the body still on different parts

Session 6: Keeping still whilst on hands and feet.
Session 7: Keeping still on knees and elbows, backs and tummies.

Unit 5 Stretching out and tucking up

Session 8: Holding stretched and tucked positions.
Session 9: Moving in stretched out and tucked up positions.
Session 10: Stretching out and tucking up whilst travelling.

YEAR 2

Spring Term

Unit 3 Using parts of the body

Session 1: To take weight whilst moving.
Session 2: To take weight whilst still.
Session 3: To transfer weight from feet to hands.
Session 4: To transfer weight from feet to hands (2).
Session 5: To transfer weight using other parts.
Session 6: To jump and land with the feet either together or apart.
Session 7: To travel on hands and feet, with the feet either together or apart.
Session 8: To slide and roll, with the feet either together or apart.
Session 9: To travel along straight lines.
Session 10: To travel along a zig-zag pathway

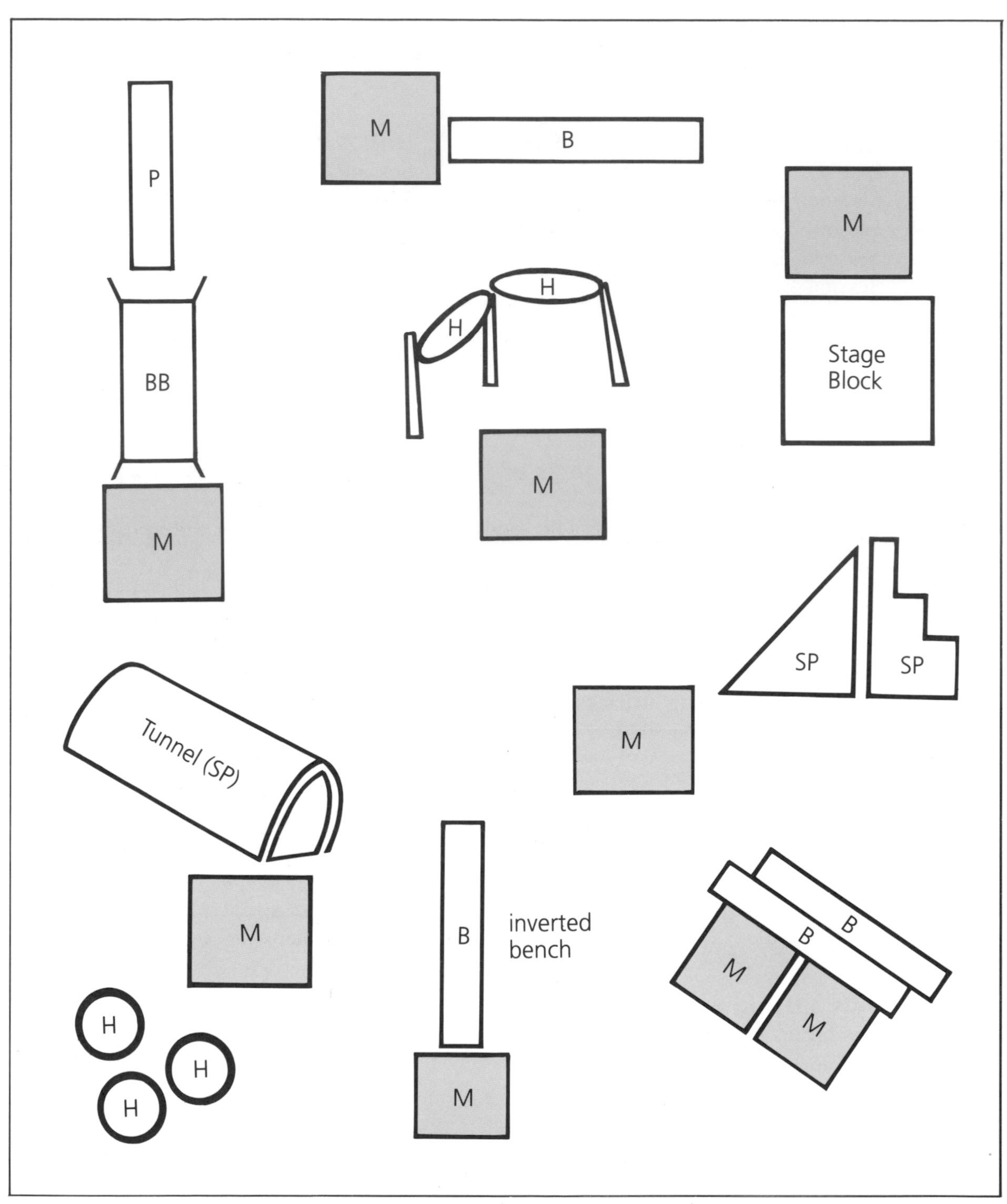

A sample apparatus plan for Recpetion incorporating soft play equipment, stage blocks, hoops placed on the floor and activity skittles.

SP = soft play equipment   H = hoop

RECEPTION: INTRODUCTION

APPARATUS
Autumn and Spring Terms.

The apparatus, suitable for the age group, should be set out before the lesson by adults. The children are encouraged to explore the apparatus freely, choosing where they go. The teacher generally sees that the children work safely, with no overcrowding, pushing etc. She should circulate amongst the children, keeping in a position where she can see them all, describing the actions they do. Where appropriate she should intervene making suggestions, encouraging and praising the children.

The layout needs to be kept fairly simple and the same layout kept for several weeks in order for the children to become familiar with it. If space is limited, then the apparatus work may have to be done in a separate lesson, in which case one or two activities should be done on the floor first in the spaces between the apparatus.

Apparatus must not be improvised but stage blocks (providing there are no staples, splinters etc.) and soft play equipment are very useful. Activity skittles, linked together with large hoops set at different angles provide interesting holes for the children to climb through, slide under and jump in and out (see Introduction).

RECEPTION

Autumn Term Session 1: NAMING THE ACTIONS
Sit, stand, walk, run

	Content	Teaching points
Warming Up	1 Sit on floor without touching anyone.	1 Do the actions with the children at first, then repeat commands without joining in the actions.
	2 STAND UP.	
	3 Stretch fingers in the air.	
Floor Work	1 WALK following the teacher.	1 Lead the children in and out of the apparatus in a circuitous route about the room verbalizing about where we are going, *e.g.* over to the piano, past the door.
	2 RUN lightly STOP on signal . . .	2 Do the actions with the children say 'and . . . stop' to give some warning of when to stop.
	3 RUN, STOP, STAND STILL	

	Content	Teaching points
Apparatus Activities	1 WALK and put your hands on a piece of apparatus.	1 Children move about the room freely, perform the actions as you give the command.
	2 WALK and put your hands on another piece of apparatus.	
	3 Choose a piece of apparatus climb on it, get off carefully.	3 Watch for over-crowding. Explain to the children that they have to take turns.
	4 WALK to another piece of apparatus, climb on it, and get off carefully.	
Calming Activity	1 STAND UP and stretch your fingers in the air. Then: Put your arms by your side.	1 Make sure all the children are away from the apparatus. If there is space gather them close to you at one end of the room.

RECEPTION

Autumn Term Session 2: NAMING THE ACTIONS
Slide, spin, push, pull

	Content	Teaching points
Warming Up	1 Sit on floor without touching anyone.	
	2 Stand up.	
	3 Run lightly anywhere, stop on signal.	3 Run with the children, saying, 'lightly, on your toes, quietly, look were you are going' etc. Run in and out of the apparatus.
Floor Work	1 Sit and SPIN round on the floor.	1 Do it with the children at first. Watch they do not get giddy.
	2 Can you SPIN round another way?	2 Articulate the different ways the children find.
	3 Lie on tummies, PULL yourselves along.	
	4 Lie on backs, PUSH yourselves along.	
	5 Find another way of sliding along.	

	Content	Teaching points
Apparatus Activities	Repeat last session's apparatus activities first to familiarize them with the apparatus.	
	1 Let the children explore the apparatus.	1 Watch for over-crowding explain that they have to take turns.
	2 Find places where you can SLIDE along.	2 Verbalize the children's responses, *eg*. 'Mary is sliding on her tummy along the plank', etc.
Calming Activity	Stand and stretch your fingers in the air. Then: Put your arms by your side.	

RECEPTION

Autumn Term Session 3: NAMING THE ACTIONS Jumping and landing

	Content	Teaching points
Warming Up	1 Sit on the floor without touching anyone.	
	2 Stand up.	
	3 Walk anywhere.	3 Encourage going all over the room, avoiding the apparatus.
	4 Run lightly and stop on signal.	4 Talk as they run encouraging them to run quietly and carefully avoiding the apparatus. Say, 'and . . . stop' to warn them in advance.
Floor Work	1 With feet together do light bouncy jumps on the spot.	1 Show the children what to do. Encourage a slight 'give' in the knees.
	2 Do light bouncy jumps about the room.	2 Watch that they keep away from the apparatus.

Content	Teaching points
3 On the spot, bend your knees, do a big jump and bend knees on landing.	3 Show the children first. Select a good example and let the children watch. Talk with them about good landings.

Apparatus Activities

Repeat session 1 Apparatus Activities first to familiarize them with the apparatus.

Content	Teaching points
1 Let the children explore the apparatus.	1 Watch for over-crowding.
2 Find places where you can jump safely off the apparatus.	2 Where possible children should jump onto mats. Explain the function of the mats. Circulate and verbalize the actions, so they begin to recognize the vocabulary.

Calming Activity

Stand and stretch your fingers in the air.

Then:
Put your arms by your side.

RECEPTION

Autumn Term Session 4: NAMING THE ACTIONS
Hopping and skipping

	Content	Teaching points
Warming Up	1 Sit on the floor without touching anyone.	
	2 Stand up.	
	3 Run lightly and stop on signal.	3 Keep talking to the children as they run, encouraging them to look for spaces, run lightly, no bumping into anything etc.
	4 Do light bouncy jumps anywhere.	4 Remind them about bending their knees slightly as they land.
Floor Work	1 HOP anywhere.	1 Keep activity short.
	2 SKIP anywhere, (No ropes).	2 Do it with them at first. Do not worry if some can not skip at this stage.

	Content	Teaching points
	3 Choose a way of travelling anywhere.	3 Give examples – 'you can run, hop, walk, skip, slide etc'. Verbalize their responses and name the actions they have chosen. Watch spacing. Select one or two for demonstration. Discuss what actions they are doing.
Apparatus Activities	1 Let them explore the apparatus.	1 Circulate and verbalize their actions.
	2 When you leave a piece of apparatus, HOP or SKIP to another piece.	2 Select a child to show what (s)he has done. Let the class name the actions (s)he has chosen to do.
Calming Activity	Stand and stretch your fingers in the air. Then: Put your arms by your side.	

RECEPTION

Autumn Term Session 5: NAMING THE ACTIONS
Rocking and rolling

Warming Up

	Content	Teaching points
1	Sit on floor without touching anyone.	
2	Stand up.	
3	Do bouncy jumps anywhere.	Watch for spacing.
4	Hop anywhere.	Keep activity short. Encourage hopping on right and left feet.
5	Skip anywhere.	

Floor Work

	Content	Teaching points
1	Sit on the floor and ROCK from side to side.	Do it with the children at first. Legs should be stretched out, feet together.
2	Stand and ROCK from foot to foot.	Show the children what you mean.

	Content	Teaching points
	3 Can you ROCK another way?	3 *ie,* on knees, tummies, backs etc. Select some good examples to show. Discuss them together and let them try to copy them.
	4 Tuck up small and roll over sideways.	4 Demonstrate using a child. Discourage covering eyes with hands.
	5 Stretch out and roll over sideways.	5 Make sure they have enough room to roll.
Apparatus Activities	1 Let the children explore the apparatus.	1 Circulate and verbalize the children's actions, so that they become familiar with the names of the actions.
	2 Find places where you can ROCK on the apparatus.	2 Highlight good examples *eg* 'Mary is rocking from foot to foot on the bench'. Select a child to demonstrate a good rocking action on the apparatus. Discuss with the children what (s)he is rocking on. What other actions is (s)he doing?
Calming Activity	Show me a way of rocking. Then: Stand up.	

RECEPTION

Autumn Term Session 6: FAMILIARIZATION WITH THE SPACE
Finding a space – magic spots

Warming Up

Content	Teaching points
1 Stand in a space.	
2 Walk anywhere, look for spaces as you walk.	2 Keep reminding the children to look for spaces.
3 Run lightly anywhere, stop in a space on signal.	3 Give the signal, 'and . . . stop'. Point out the empty spaces when they have stopped.

Floor Work

Content	Teaching points
1 Stand on a spot.	1 Help the children to recognize their spots – maybe a scuff mark on the floor, for example.
2 Walk anywhere, return to your magic spot.	
3 Run anywhere, on signal return to your magic spot.	
4 Jump up and down on your magic spot.	
5 Choose a way of travelling anywhere, on signal return to your magic spot and sit on it.	5 Discourage rushing quickly back to magic spot – it is not a race.

	Content	Teaching points
Apparatus Activities	1. Let the children explore the apparatus.	
	2 Stand on a magic spot near the apparatus and return to your magic spot when you have finished.	2 Help the children to find suitable magic spots near their apparatus, make sure they return to the same spot. Spots can be scattered around the apparatus, thus avoiding waiting in a queue. Select a good example for all to watch. Discuss with them what actions they saw, where they were being performed etc.
Calming Activity	1 Stand on your spot and stretch your arms up high.	1 Can they find their original magic spots?
	2 Sit quietly on your magic spot.	
	Then: Stand up.	

RECEPTION

Autumn Term Session 7: FAMILIARIZATION WITH THE SPACE

Moving to a new space.

	Content	Teaching points
Warming Up	1 Sit on your magic spot.	
	2 Stand and stretch your arms high in the air.	2. Circulate and encourage a full stretch.
	3 Stretch one leg out and then the other.	3 Show the children first, encourage a full stretch.
Floor Work	1 Stand on your magic spot, walk to a new space and stand still.	1 Children return to magic spots after each activity.
	2 Run lightly into a different space and stand still.	2 Check that they have run into a space. Those not in a space – explain what you mean.
	3 Slide into a new space then sit down.	3 Watch they have room to slide.
	4 Choose a way of travelling into a new space and then sit down.	4 Select a good demonstration. Ask the children to name the way of travelling chosen.

	Content	Teaching points
Apparatus Activities	1 Let the children explore the apparatus.	
	2 Find new spaces on the apparatus to move into.	2 As the children work, circulate and remind them to look for spaces to move into. Continue to verbalize the actions, *eg*. 'John is sliding into a new space'.
Calming Activity	1 Stand quietly in a space.	

RECEPTION

Autumn Term Session 8: **FAMILIARIZATION WITH THE SPACE**
Stopping in a space

	Content	Teaching points
Warming Up	1 Stand on your magic spot.	1 Help children to recognize their spots. They need not be the same ones as in previous lessons.
	2 Hop anywhere, on signal return to magic spot.	
Floor Work	1 Walk anywhere, on signal look for a space and stop in that space.	1 Say, 'look for a space and... stop'. Walk round and praise those who are in a space.
	2 Run lightly anywhere, on signal look for a different space and stop.	
	3 Choose another way of travelling anywhere, on signal stop in a space.	3 Select a good demonstration. Ask the children to name the way of travelling chosen. 'Did (s)he stop in a space?'

	Content	Teaching points
Apparatus Activities	1 Let the children explore the apparatus.	
	2 Find spaces on the apparatus where you can stop and then move on again.	2 Circulate and ask the children , 'Where are you going to stop?' Select a good demonstration. Ask the children to tell you where (s)he stopped, and what actions (s)he was doing.
	3 Stand on a magic spot near the apparatus, travel on the apparatus and return to your magic spot when you have finished.	
Calming Activity	1 Walk anywhere, stop in a space and tuck up small.	1 Circulate, checking that the children really are small with arms and legs tucked tightly around the centre of the body.
	2 Stand quietly.	

RECEPTION

Autumn Term Session 9: FAMILIARIZATION WITH THE SPACE

Big spaces

	Content	Teaching points
Warming Up	1 Stand in a space. 2 Jump lightly up and down in that space. 3 Walk to a new space. 4 Sit and spin round in that new space.	These activities should be done three times. The first time the teacher should do it with them, the second verbalizing only and the third time the children ought to be able to do them unaided.
Floor Work	1 Walk anywhere taking BIG steps, and looking for BIG spaces.	1 Demonstrate big steps at first.
	2 Half the class stand still in BIG spaces, the rest walk in and out of them taking BIG steps and looking for BIG spaces in which to walk.	2 Those standing still can be like 'lamp posts' and the rest walk in and out of the 'lamp posts'. Check the 'lamp posts' are well spread out.
	3 Change over.	
	4 Half the class stand still as before. Find ways of doing BIG movements in and out of each other.	

	Content	Teaching points
Apparatus Activities	1 Look for BIG spaces whilst moving on the apparatus.	1 *ie*, places where there are no other children, or where there is a space above them, or in a space under the apparatus.
	2 Can you make yourself BIG as you move on the apparatus?	2 Circulate and name the children who are trying to make themselves big, *eg* 'Tommy is really big on the climbing frame'
Calming Activity	Find a BIG space and stand in it, how BIG can you make yourself? Stand up.	

RECEPTION

Autumn Term Session 10: FAMILIARIZATION WITH THE SPACE

Small spaces

	Content	Teaching points
Warming Up	1 Stand in a space. 2 Hop to a new space.	These activities should be done three times, the first time the teacher should do it with them, the second time verbalizing only, and the third time the children ought to be able to do them unaided.
	3 Skip to another space. 4 Sit and spin round in a space.	
Floor Work	1 Walk in and out of each other. How close can you walk to each other without touching?	1 Explain that by being close to each other they are taking up a small space.
	2 Stand in a space. Walk very close to someone else and stand near them.	

	Content	Teaching points
	3 Half the class stand still fairly close to each other. The rest walk in and out of them without touching.	3 Those standing still act as 'lamp posts'.
	4 Change over.	
	5 Make yourself small, find a way of moving to a new space.	5 Select a demonstration, discuss with the children now (s)he made herself/ himself small, taking up a small space, and what actions (s)he chose to do.
Apparatus Activities	1 Look for small spaces whilst moving on the apparatus.	
	2 Find places where you can be small whilst moving on the apparatus.	
	3 Sometimes make yourself make yourself big and sometimes small whilst moving on the apparatus.	3 Circulate and ask the children, 'Are you being big or small?' 'What action are you doing?' etc.
Calming Activity	1 Sit on the floor close to one another without touching. Stand up.	

RECEPTION

Autumn Term ASSESSMENT AND CONSOLIDATION SESSION

The children by now should begin to:-

1 Be familiar with the procedure of undressing, walking to the hall, working quietly and returning to the classroom, etc.,

2 Respond to commands,

3 Know the names of the actions and be able to talk about what they and other children are doing,

4 Become familiar with the apparatus and explore it with confidence,

5 Understand what we mean by ‘look for a space’ and become aware of obstacles and other children when they are moving about.

If the teacher feels more time is needed on any aspect (s)he can use this session to consolidate the work.

For your notes and comments

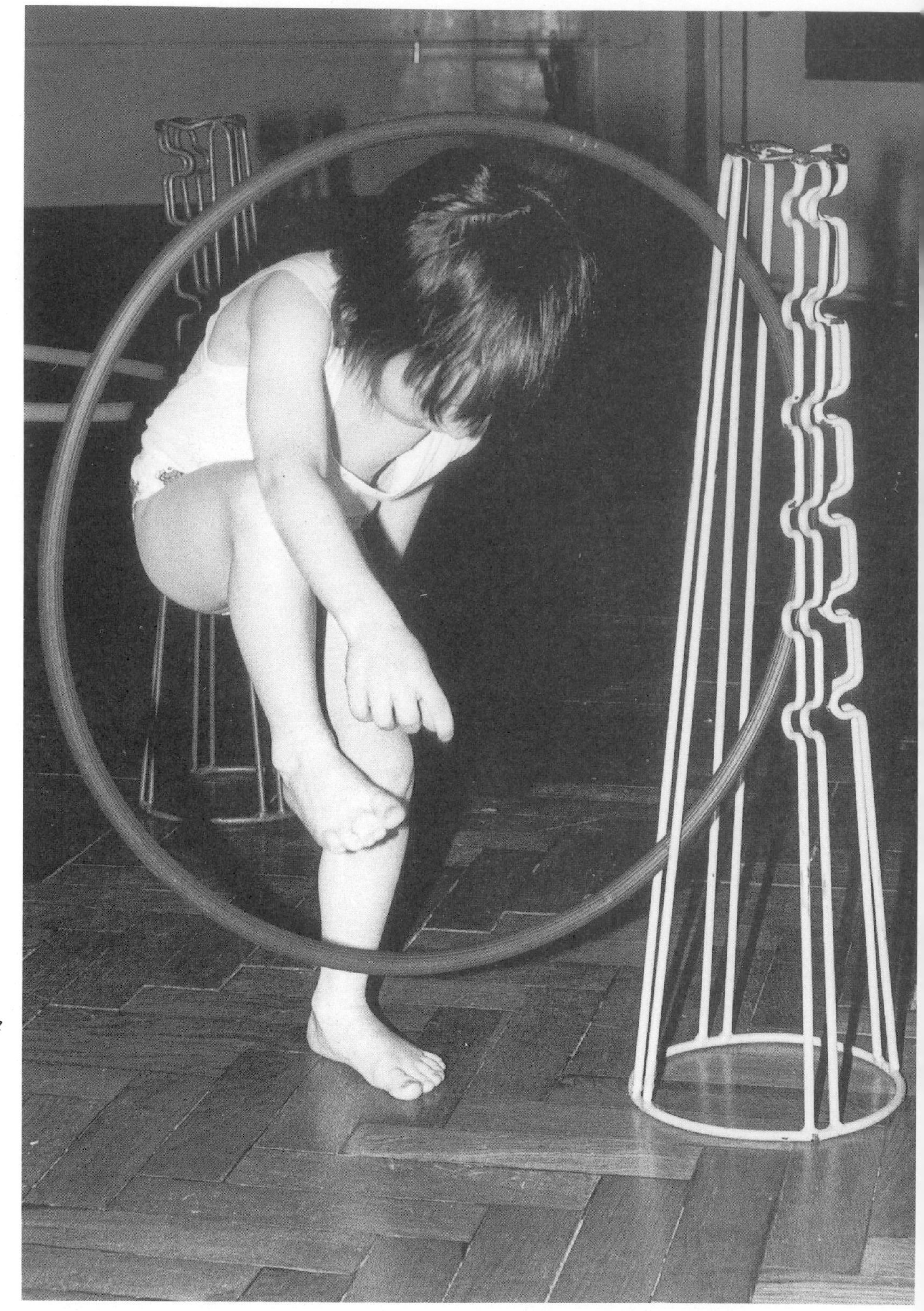

Find places where you can be small whilst moving on the apparatus, (Session 10 Autumn term).

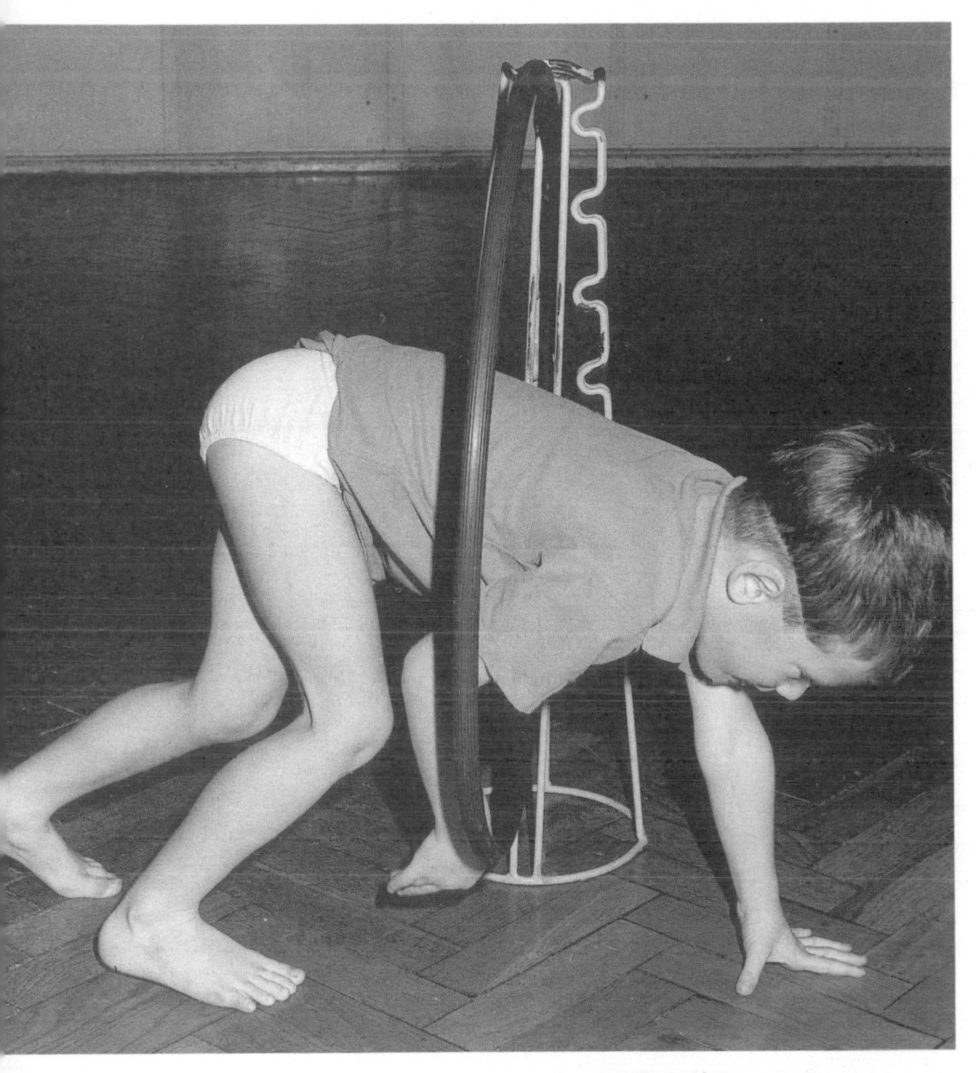

Activity Skittles, linked together with large hoops set at different angles provide interesting holes for the children to climb through. (Autumn and Spring terms).

RECEPTION

Spring Term Session 1: IDENTIFYING PARTS OF THE BODY
Feet and hands (1)

	Content	Teaching points
Warming Up	1 Stand in a space and stretch your hands above your head.	1 Circulate and encourage full extension of arms and fingers.
	2 Stand on tip toes.	
	3 Shake your fingers.	
	4 Sit and shake your feet.	4 Do this with the children.
Floor Work	1 Walk on your tip toes.	Do these activities with the children at first, then walk around them encouraging them and talking to them. *eg*. 'Peter has very big hands'.
	2 Walk on your heels.	
	3 Can you walk on the insides and outsides of your feet?	
	4 Make your hands big.	

	Content	Teaching points
	5 Put your big hands on the floor, and walk your feet around them.	
	6 Sit and make your hands into fists.	
	7 Punch strongly into the air with your fists.	
Apparatus Activities	1 Let the children explore the apparatus.	Circulate and talk generally to the class as they work. *eg.* 'Mary is using her feet to climb up the ladder'.
	2 Find ways of using your feet and hands on the apparatus.	
Calming Activity	1 Lie on your backs in a space. Stretch your hands and feet in the air.	
	2 Stand up quietly.	

RECEPTION

Spring Term Session 2: IDENTIFYING PARTS OF THE BODY
Feet and hands (2)

	Content	Teaching points
Warming Up	1 Walk anywhere on tip toes.	
	2 Walk anywhere on tip toes with your hands stretched high in the air.	
	3 Find different ways of walking.	3 Articulate the responses. *eg.* 'Ann is taking big steps'. Select some interesting examples for the class to watch and try to copy. Talk with them about the examples.
Floor Work	1 Make big hands.	
	2 Put your big hands on the floor, and jump your feet around them.	
	3 Sit on the floor and stretch hands and feet in the air.	
	4 Find other ways of stretching your hands and feet in the air.	4 Select some interesting examples for the rest to watch. Ask the children to tell you what they saw.

	Content	Teaching points
Apparatus Activities	1 Let the children explore the apparatus.	
	2 Find ways to use your hands to grip the apparatus.	2 Circulate and highlight good examples, *eg*. 'Peter has found a good way to grip the plank as he slides along'.
Calming Activity	Lie on your tummy and stretch your feet and hands.	Watch spacing.
	Stand up.	

RECEPTION

Spring Term Session 3: IDENTIFYING PARTS OF THE BODY
Arms and legs (1)

	Content	Teaching points
Warming Up	1 Walk anywhere on tip toes.	
	2 Walk anywhere stretching out your legs.	
	3 Stand and circle your arms.	3 Watch spacing. Circle arms slowly, close to the ears.
Floor Work	1 Put your hands on the floor and try to travel along with straight arms and legs.	1 Select a good example for the class to watch.
	2 Find other ways of travelling with straight arms and legs.	2 Select some examples for the class to watch. Discuss what they have seen, highlighting what the arms and legs are doing.

	Content	Teaching points
Apparatus Activities	1 Let the children explore the apparatus.	
	2 Find places where you can stretch your arms and legs.	
	3 Roll sideways on the mats after you have been on a piece of apparatus.	3 Circulate and ensure the children roll *sideways*.
Calming Activity	Stand still with your arms stretched by your sides.	

RECEPTION

Spring Term Session 4: IDENTIFYING PARTS OF THE BODY
Arms and legs (2)

	Content	Teaching points
Warming Up	1 Walk anywhere with your legs crossed.	
	2 Jump up and down on the spot with your arms stretched in the air.	2 Ensure the children are spread out. Give in the knees on take-off and landing.
	3 Stand and circle your arms.	3 Slowly, close to ears.
Floor Work	1 Roll sideways with your arms and legs tucked up.	1 Discourage the children from covering their eyes with their hands. Select a good example for the rest to watch. Discuss how (s)he has tucked in the arms and legs. Use mats if preferred.
	2 In a crouch position, jump anywhere with your legs bent.	
	3 Find other ways of travelling with your legs bent.	3 Look at a few examples, get the children to tell you what they have seen.

	Content	Teaching points
Apparatus Activities	1 Let the children explore the apparatus.	
	2 Find places where you can move with your legs straight.	2 Circulate and verbalize the responses, *eg*. 'Peter has found a way of sliding with his legs straight'.
	3 Find places where you can move with legs bent.	
	4 Find places where you can move with your arms stretched high in the air.	
	5 Roll *sideways* on the mats after you have been on the apparatus, sometimes with your arms and legs straight and sometimes with them tucked up.	
Calming Activity	Stand and stretch your arms high in the air. Then: stand up straight.	

RECEPTION

Spring Term Session 5: IDENTIFYING PARTS OF THE BODY
Backs, tummies and heads

	Content	Teaching points
Warming Up	1 On hands and feet wag your tail like a dog.	1 Make sure the children are on their feet and not their knees.
	2 On hands and feet arch your back. (Happy cat/angry cat).	
	3 Walk anywhere with your head stretched high.	
Floor Work	1 Can you slide on your back?	1 Watch spacing.
	2 Can you slide on your tummy?	
	3 Lie on your back and stretch your legs in the air.	3 Circulate and encourage a full extension of the legs. Keep the activity short.
	4 Stand and put your head between your knees.	4 Look through your legs like a clown does. Ask 'What can you see?'

	Content	Teaching points
Apparatus Activities	1 Let the children explore the apparatus.	
	2 Can you stretch your head high on the apparatus?	2 Circulate and highlight good examples as the children are working, *eg*. 'Mary is stretching her head really high as she walks along the bench'.
Calming Activity	Lie on your back or tummy. Keep very still. Then: Stand up.	

RECEPTION

Spring Term Session 6: IDENTIFYING PARTS OF THE BODY
Knees and elbows

	Content	Teaching points
Warming Up	1 Kneel on the floor and circle your arms.	1 Slowly, close to the ears. Keep the activity short.
	2 Kneel and touch the floor lightly with your elbows.	2 One after the other.
	3 Walk anywhere lifting your knees high.	
	4 Run anywhere lifting your knees high.	4 Watch spacing.
Floor Work	1 Can you balance on your knees and elbows on the mats?	1 Move the mats away from the apparatus into spaces.
	2 Roll sideways, tucked up with knees and elbows touching.	2 Children may have to take turns.
	3 Do bouncy jumps across the mat lifting your knees high.	

	Content	Teaching points
	4 Find other ways of crossing the mats on your knees and elbows.	4 Select a good demonstration discuss with the children what they have seen. Remember to replace the mats.
Apparatus Activities	1 Let the children explore the apparatus.	
	2 Find places where you can go on your knees and elbows.	2 Circulate and identify any movements in which knees and elbows are involved.
Calming Activity	Sit crossed-legged, fold your arms try to stand up. Stand very still.	

RECEPTION

Spring Term Session 7: POSITIONAL LANGUAGE On and off

	Content	Teaching points
Warming Up	1 Stand ON a mat.	1 Move the mats away from the apparatus into spaces.
	2 Walk anywhere, on a signal stand ON a mat.	
	3 Jump ON a mat.	
Floor Work	1 Make up a jumpy pattern ON a mat.	1 Select some good examples for the class to watch and try to copy. Discuss what we mean by a pattern.
	2 Make up a jumpy pattern jumping ON and OFF a mat.	
	3 Travel round the mat with your hands ON it and your feet OFF it.	
	4 Roll over sideways ON the mat.	4 Tucked up or stretched out. Remember to replace the mats.

	Content	Teaching points
Apparatus Activities	1 Let the children explore the apparatus.	
	2 Get ON and OFF the apparatus then jump ON and OFF the mat.	2 Circulate and verbalize the responses, *eg*. 'Jane has found a good way of climbing ON the apparatus'. Select an example, let the class watch and discuss with the children what they have seen.
Calming Activity	Sit ON a mat and keep very still. Then: Stand up.	

RECEPTION

Spring Term Session 8: POSITIONAL LANGUAGE
Under and over

	Content	Teaching points
Warming Up	1 Walk anywhere, step OVER the corner of a mat.	1 Move the mats away from the apparatus into spaces. Show the children what to do.
	2 Walk anywhere, jump OVER the corner of a mat.	
Floor Work	1 Make up a pattern going OVER the mats.	1 Discuss with the children first what movements they could do.
	2 Half the class lie down in spaces, the rest step OVER them very carefully.	2 On the floor or on the mats. Those lying down MUST keep still. Remember to change over.
	3 Half the class make bridges with weight on hands and feet. The rest slide UNDER them very carefully.	3 Watch there is no strain on their backs (as in a crab). Do this on the floor, it is easier to slide. Remember to replace the mats.

	Content	Teaching points
Apparatus Activities	1 Let the children explore the apparatus.	
	2 Walk anywhere. Find places where you can slide UNDER the apparatus.	2 Select a few examples for the class to watch. Stress the fact that the children are going UNDER the apparatus.
	3 Walk anywhere. Find places where you can step OVER the apparatus.	3 Check that the children choose places where in fact they can step over. Keep this activity short.
Calming Activity	Lie down on your backs, keep very still. Then: Stand up.	

RECEPTION

Spring Term Session 9: POSITIONAL LANGUAGE
In and out

	Content	Teaching points
Warming Up	1 Walk IN and OUT of each other.	1 Ask the children, 'What do we mean by going in and out?'
	2 Run IN and OUT of each other.	
	3 Jump IN and OUT of each other.	3 Give slightly in the knees on take-off and landing.
Floor Work	1 Find other ways of going IN and OUT of each other.	1 Give help with finding different ways, *eg* sliding, hopping etc.
	2 Half the class stand still in spaces, the rest find other ways of going IN and OUT of each other.	2 Remember to change over.
	3 Half the class stand still in spaces, the rest find other ways of going IN and OUT of each other.	3 Ask those who have been standing still to tell you what ways the other children found to go in and out. Remember to change over.

	Content	Teaching points
Apparatus Activities	1 Walk IN and OUT of the apparatus without touching it.	
	2 Let the children explore the apparatus.	
Calming Activity	Walk quietly IN and OUT of each other. Stand very still.	

RECEPTION

Spring Term Session 10: POSITIONAL LANGUAGE

Along and across

NB Skipping ropes (preferably without handles) will be needed in this session.

	Content	Teaching points
Warming Up	1 Walk anywhere, stop on signal.	1 Say, 'and . . . stop'.
	2 Run anywhere, stop on signal.	2 Talk to the children about how to stop, so grip tightly with arms, legs, tummies etc.
	3 Stand and circle your arms.	3 Slowly, close to ears.
	4 Get a skipping rope.	
	5 Skip with your rope.	5 Watch spacing if apparatus is out. Those who find this difficult could be helped in a games lesson.
Floor Work	1 Place rope on the floor in a line.	
	2 Walk ALONG the rope.	
	3 Jump ALONG the rope.	

	Content	Teaching points
	4 Find other ways of going ALONG the rope.	4 Select a few examples, *eg*. going along on hands and feet, for the class to watch and try to copy. Discuss with the children what they have seen.
	5 Find ways of going ACROSS the rope.	
	6 Put your rope away.	
Apparatus Activities	1 Let the children explore the apparatus.	
	2 Find ways of going ACROSS the apparatus.	2 Circulate and suggest ways they could go across the apparatus. Select one or two examples for the rest to watch. Discuss with the children what they have seen.
Calming Activity	Lie down on your back. Keep very still. Then: Stand up.	

RECEPTION

Spring Term ASSESSMENT AND CONSOLIDATION SESSION.

The children by now should:

1 Know the procedure of a Gymnastics lesson.

2 Be able to listen to simple instructions, and respond physically to verbal commands.

3 Recognize and know the names of basic actions.

4 Be familiar with the surrounding space and able to use it to good advantage, without bumping into each other or into apparatus which is put out in readiness for use later in the lesson.

5 Be consciously aware of specific parts of the body.

6 Understand the meaning of prepositional language through movement, such as on and off etc.

7 Be able to talk about what they are doing in the lesson.

8 Be able to observe and recognize what movements other children do.

9 Be able to copy what movements the teacher and other children do.

10 Be conscious of what they are doing on the apparatus and able to verbalize about what movements they do, and how they use it.

If the teacher feels more time is needed on any aspect she can use this session to consolidate the work.

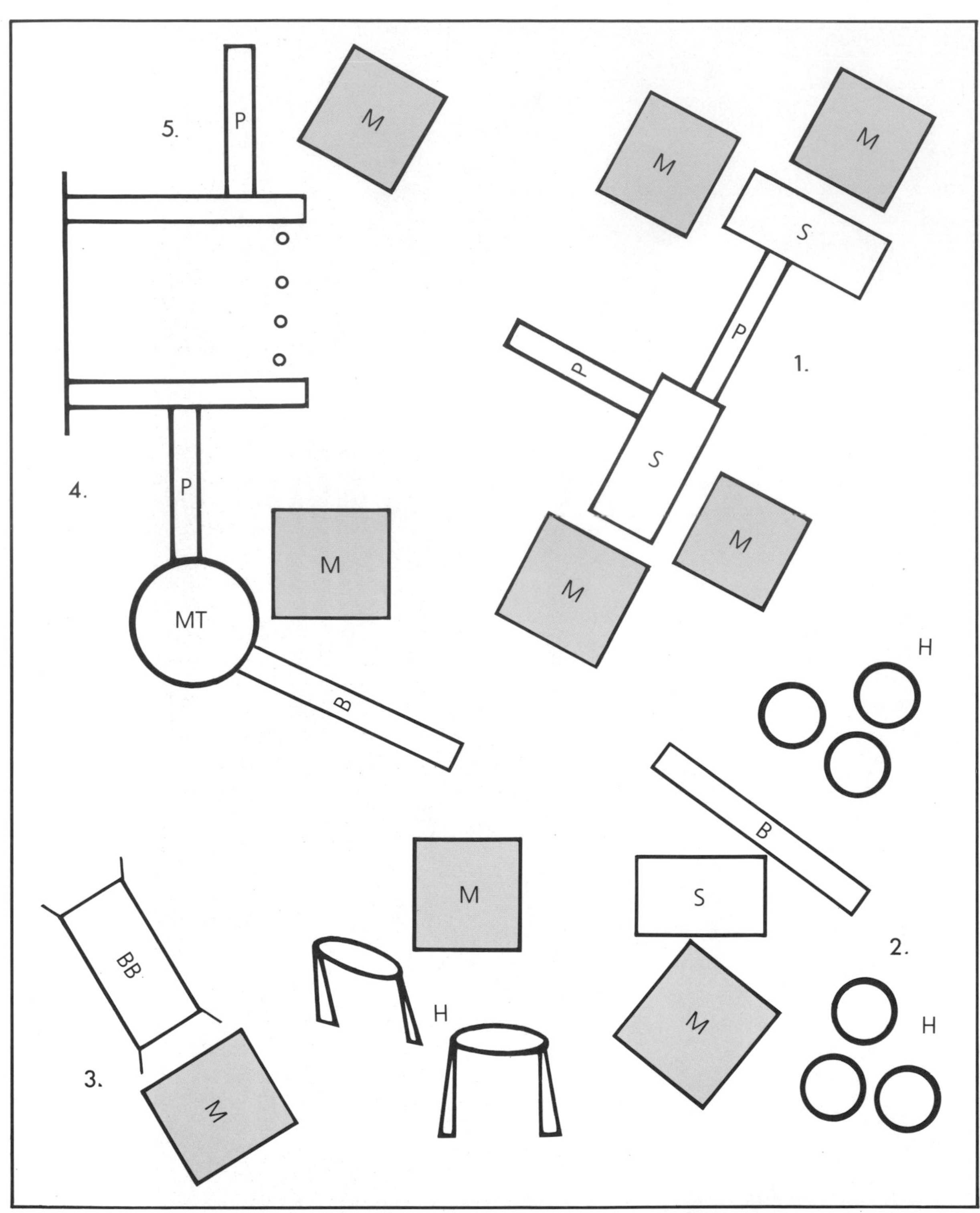

A sample apparatus pattern for Year 1, incorporating hoops placed on the floor and hoops supported on activity skittles.

YEAR 1: INTRODUCTION

APPARATUS
Autumn Term

Benches, low agility and/or movement tables, box tops and other low apparatus with large surfaces, and mats, will be used this term. These should be placed in readiness around the sides of the room if possible, and the children taught how to lift each piece into position. This can be introduced gradually so that by half term they are able to put all the required apparatus into position and replace it at the sides of the room after use. It saves time if the same children move the same piece of apparatus each lesson. They can learn how to move other pieces next term. The layout should be the same each lesson.

If time is short then the activities leading to work on the apparatus can be taught in a separate lesson. The warming up activities should still be done, and before going onto the apparatus the children should be reminded of the unit they are working on and the specific relevant emphasis (*eg*. Being Aware of the Space – high and low).

Children should be placed in five or six groups. Each group should be allocated a 'station', *ie*. a layout of two or three pieces of apparatus. After working at one station for a few minutes the teacher should stop them and keeping in their groups, the children should walk to the next 'station' and begin work. At the end of the lesson she should note which 'station' each group has arrived at so the children can begin work there next lesson before moving on again. (Two groups can be accommodated on the climbing frame.)

In most instances there are simple tasks for the children to concentrate on whilst on the apparatus. There are also some more complicated tasks involving more complex sequencing. It will depend on the time available, the apparatus, space and ability of the children as to whether all the tasks are attempted.

YEAR 1

Autumn Term Session 1: BEING AWARE OF THE ACTIONS
Going and stopping

	Content	Teaching points
Warming Up	1 Walk anywhere, stop on signal.	1 Say 'and . . . stop.' Discuss with the children how to stop, *eg*. one foot in front of the other, knees slightly bent, grip with the muscles and freeze.
	2 Run anywhere, stop on signal.	
	3 Stand and stretch your arms up in the air.	
	4 Stretch one leg out and then the other.	
Floor Work	1 Find your own way of going along.	1 Make suggestions – see previous activities in Reception sessions. Circulate and name actions, *eg*. 'Paul is sliding' etc.
	2 Go along a little way then stop.	2 Select a good example for the class to watch. Ask 'How did (s)he go along?'
	3 Go along one way, stop then go along again a different way.	3 If necessary, ask them to count up to five when they have stopped before going along again.

	Content	Teaching points
Apparatus Activities	See notes on page 63.	
	1 Find a way of going along the apparatus and across the mats.	
	2 On the apparatus, go along a little way, stop then carry on.	
	3 Start on the floor, travel up to the apparatus, go on it get off and go across the mat.	3 The children may need help with where to start. Encourage different ways of going by making suggestions and asking the children to make suggestions.
	4 Start on the floor, travel up to the apparatus, go on it get off it and go across the mat. Find a way of getting back to where you started.	4 Select an example for the class to watch. Discuss with the children what actions they saw.
	5 Put the apparatus away.	
Calming Activity	Lie down quietly on your backs. Then: Stand up.	

YEAR 1

Autumn Term Session 2:

BEING AWARE OF THE ACTIONS

Slide, spin, push, pull

(This can be split, i.e. one session on sliding and spinning and one session on pushing and pulling)

	Content	Teaching points
Warming Up	1 Walk anywhere. Stop on signal.	
	2 Run anywhere, stop when you choose, then carry on running.	2 Watch to see they do, in fact stop. They may be expecting a command.
	3 Find another way of going along.	3 Select one or two examples for the rest to watch and try to copy. Discuss with them what actions they saw.
Floor Work	1 Find ways of spinning round.	1 Watch spacing. Keep activity short. Articulate the responses.
	2 Can you slide along on your tummy?	
	3 Find other ways of sliding.	3 *eg*. on backs, sides etc. Select examples as before.
	4 Use your hands to push yourself along on your back.	
	5 Use your heels to help you slide along on your back.	

	Content	Teaching points
Apparatus Activities	See notes on page 63.	
	1 Find places where you can slide.	1 Circulate and comment on what you see, *eg*. 'Mary is sliding on her tummy'.
	2 Spin round on the floor, then slide on the apparatus.	
	3 Find places where you can push or pull yourself along.	3 Select an example for the class to watch. Discuss with the children what they have seen.
	4 Put the apparatus away.	
Calming Activity	Sit on the floor, spin round once then lie down quietly.	
	Then: Stand up.	

Use your heels to help you slide along on your back.

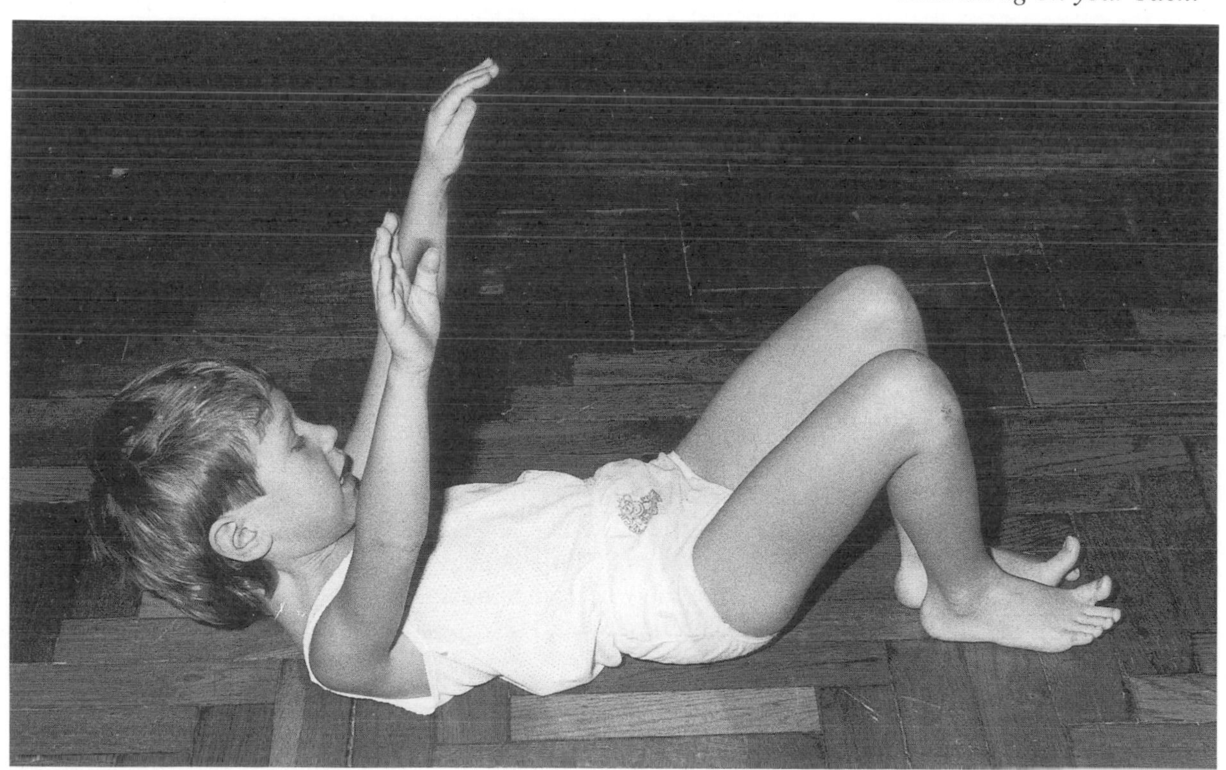

YEAR 1

Autumn Term Session 3: BEING AWARE OF THE ACTIONS
Jumping and landing

	Content	Teaching points
Warming Up	1 Walk anywhere. Stop on signal.	1 *Eg*. 'and . . . . stop'.
	2 Run lightly in and out of each other.	2 Encourage soft placing of the feet on the floor.
Floor Work	1 Do little bouncy jumps anywhere.	1 Keep feet together, bend the knees slightly on take-off and landing – resilient jumps like a bouncing ball (see **Specific Skills Guide**).
	2 From bent knees spring high into the air and bend your knees on landing.	2 The emphasis is on the spring UP.
	3 Sometimes do little bouncy jumps anywhere, then do a big springy jump.	3 Select an example for the class to watch. Ask 'Where did (s)he do a big springy jump?' Stress the difference between the two kinds of jump.

	Content	Teaching points
Apparatus Activities	See notes on page 63.	
	1 Explore the apparatus and find places where you can jump off it.	1 Children should land in the centre of the mat on their feet, with bent knees. If necessary, the hands can be placed on the mats in front of them for support. They should not land on their knees.
	2 Start on the floor in a space. Do bouncy jumps up to the apparatus, move on it, jump off then do bouncy jumps back to where you started.	
	3 Put the apparatus away.	
Calming Activity	All do 'Jack-in-a-Box' together. Then: Stand up.	Start in a crouched position. All say, 'Jack-in-a-Box jumps up like . . . THIS'. On the word THIS, all do a big, springy jump and land in a crouched position again.

YEAR 1

Autumn Term Session 4: BEING AWARE OF THE ACTIONS

Hopping and skipping (without ropes)

	Content	Teaching points
Warming Up	1 With your feet together, do light bouncy jumps anywhere.	1 Slight 'give' in the knees on take-off and landing. Resilient jumps – like a ball.
	2 Do four springy jumps on the spot.	2 Emphasis on the springing UP.
	3 Do four springy jumps, stop and then do four more.	3 Count up to four when you stop before jumping again.
Floor Work	1 Hop anywhere.	
	2 Find other ways of hopping.	2 *Eg*. backwards, holding the free foot, turning round etc. Select a few examples for the class to watch and try to copy. Discuss with the children what they have seen.
	3 Find different ways of skipping.	
	4 Make up a pattern to include bouncy jumps, hopping and skipping.	

	Content	Teaching points
Apparatus Activities	See notes on page 63.	
	1 As you use the apparatus find places where you can hop.	1 *Eg*. along a bench.
	2 As you use the apparatus find places where you can skip.	2 *Eg*. along a box top.
	3 Include bouncy jumps and springy jumps when you have your go on the apparatus.	3 Select an example for the class to watch. Discuss with the children what they have seen.
	4 Put thc apparatus away.	
Calming Activity	Walk anywhere, stop, lie down quietly. Then: Stand up.	

YEAR 1

Autumn Term Session 5: BEING AWARE OF THE ACTIONS
Rocking and Rolling

	Content	Teaching points
Warming Up	1 Stand and stretch your arms.	
	2 Stretch one leg and then the other.	2 Stretch arms to assist balance.
	3 Run quietly anywhere.	3 Encourage placing feet down softly, children to think about what they are doing, not racing.
Floor Work	1 Get the mats out, put in spaces.	
	2 Sit on the mat, legs out straight, rock from side to side.	2 Keep hands in the air.
	3 Choose two parts of your body and rock from one to the other.	3 Select a few examples for the class to watch, and try to copy. Ask, 'What do we mean by rocking?'
	4 Roll sideways along the mat tucked up.	4 Discourage covering the eyes.

	Content	Teaching points
	5 Roll sideways along the mat stretched out.	
	6 Choose whether you roll along the mat stretched out or tucked up.	
	7 Lie at the end of the mat, rock from side to side, then roll sideways along the mat.	
Apparatus Activities	See notes on page 63.	
	1 As you use the apparatus, find places where you can rock from one part of your body to another.	1 Circulate and verbalize the children's responses, *eg.* 'Jane is rocking from foot to foot on the top of the box'.
	2 Travel on your apparatus, find somewhere to rock from one part of your body to another, get off and roll sideways across the mat.	2 Select an example for the class to watch. Ask the children what they saw.
	3 Put the apparatus away.	
Calming Activity	1 Sit down with your legs straight. All try to rock from side to side keeping together. Then: Stand up.	1 Say, '. . . rock and rock and rock . . . .' slowly.

YEAR 1

Autumn Term Session 6: **BEING AWARE OF THE SPACE**
Moving in and out of each other (refer to page 56)

	Content	Teaching points
Warming Up	1 Walk in and out of each other.	1 Demonstrate by walking in and out of the children.
	2 Run lightly in and out of each other.	
	3 Do bouncy jumps in and out of each other.	3 Bend knees slightly on take-off and landing.
Floor Work	1 Find a way of going in and out of each other.	1 Discuss possibilities first, *eg.* hopping, sliding etc.
	2 Find a magic spot, travel in and out of each other and back to your magic spot.	2 Select one or two examples for the rest of the class to watch. Discuss with the children what they saw. (Magic spots – see Reception, Autumn Term, Session 6).
	3 Start on your magic spot, do bouncy jumps in and out of each other and back to your magic spot.	

	Content	Teaching points
Apparatus Activities	See notes on page 63.	
	1 Walk in and out of the apparatus without touching it.	
	2 Find other ways of travelling in and out of the apparatus without touching it.	2 Refer to previous activities.
	3 Choose a magic spot in a space, travel up to the apparatus, move on it, get off, and travel a different way back to your magic spot.	
	4 Put the apparatus away.	
Calming Activity	Walk quietly in and out of each other, stop and stand still.	

YEAR 1

Autumn Term Session 7: **BEING AWARE OF THE SPACE**
Big and small

	Content	Teaching points
Warming Up	1 Walk in and out of each other.	1 Remind children what we mean by 'in and out'.
	2 Run lightly in and out of each other.	
	3 Find another way of moving in and out of each other.	3 Get children to suggest ways first.
Floor Work	1 Walk anywhere taking BIG steps.	1 Encourage putting the feet down quietly.
	2 Walk anywhere taking SMALL steps.	
	3 Find a way of travelling making yourself BIG.	3 Explain that by being big you take up a big space.
	4 Find a way of travelling making yourself SMALL.	
	5 Choose whether you are BIG or SMALL as you travel.	5 Select a few examples for the rest of the class to watch. Discuss with the children what they saw.

	Content	Teaching points
Apparatus Activities	See notes on page 63; include the climbing frame	
	1 As you use the apparatus find places where you can be BIG.	1 Circulate and comment on what you see, *eg*. 'Tom is very big on the climbing frame'.
	2 As you use the apparatus find places where you can be SMALL.	
	3 As you use the apparatus choose whether you are BIG or SMALL.	3 Select one or two examples for the class to watch. Discuss with the children what they saw.
	4 Put the apparatus away.	
Calming Activity	Find a space and tuck up small. Then: Stand up.	

YEAR 1

Autumn Term Session 8: BEING AWARE OF THE SPACE
High and low

	Content	Teaching points
Warming Up	1 Walk in and out of each other.	
	2 Walk anywhere, taking big steps.	2 Watch spacing.
	3 Do small jumps in and out of each other.	3 Bend knees on take-off and landing.
Floor Work	1 Walk and lift your legs HIGH as you go.	
	2 Walk LOW near the floor.	2 *ie*. bend knees.
	3 On the spot, spring HIGH in the air.	3 Bend knees on take-off and landing.
	4 Can you jump LOW near the floor?	4 Begin crouched.
	5 Find another way of travelling LOW near the floor.	5 Ask the children for suggestions first. Select one or two examples for the rest of the class to watch and try. Discuss with the children what they saw.

Apparatus Activities

Content

See notes on page 63; include the climbing frame

1 As you use the apparatus find places where you can be HIGH up.

2 As you use the apparatus find places where you can be LOW DOWN.

3 Choose whether you are HIGH UP or LOW DOWN when you use the apparatus.

4 Put the apparatus away.

Teaching points

1 Circulate and verbalize the children's responses, *eg.* 'Jane is really high on the climbing frame'.

3 Select one or two examples for the children to watch. Discuss with them what they have seen.

Calming Activity

Stand in a space and stretch your fingers HIGH.

Then:
Stand still.

As you use the apparatus find places where you can be low down.

YEAR 1

Autumn Term Session 9: BEING AWARE OF THE SPACE
Up to and away from

	Content	Teaching points
Warming Up	1 Walk anywhere on tip-toes.	
	2 Run lightly in and out of each other.	
	3 Do springy jumps on the spot.	3 Bend knees slightly on take-off and landing. Encourage a good spring – push your body up into the air.
Floor Work	1 Start at one end of the room. Walk UP TO to the other end.	1 This is not a race.
	2 Start at one end of the room. Find a way of travelling UP TO the other end.	2 Ask the children for suggestions first. Watch spacing. Do not let them all go at once.
	3 Start next to a partner. Walk on tip-toes AWAY FROM her.	3 Show the children what to do.
	4 Start close to the teacher. Hop AWAY FROM her.	

	Content	Teaching points
	5 With a partner, travel AWAY FROM her, then travel UP TO her a different way.	5 Select a good example for the class to watch. Discuss with the children what they have seen.
Apparatus Activities	See notes on page 63; include the climbing frame	
	1 Start AWAY FROM the apparatus, travel UP TO it in some way, then move on it.	1 Encourage the children to think of interesting movements to do up to the apparatus other than walking.
	2 Move on the apparatus, then find a way of travelling AWAY FROM it.	
	3 Find a magic spot on the floor. Travel UP TO the apparatus one way, move on it, then travel back to your magic spot another way.	3 Select one or two examples for the class to watch. Ask the children to tell you what movements they have just seen.
	4 Put the apparatus away.	
Calming Activity	All start close to each other. Move AWAY FROM each other, into a space, quietly on tip-toes. Sit down.	

YEAR 1

Autumn Term Session 10: BEING AWARE OF THE SPACE
Wide and narrow

	Content	Teaching points
Warming Up	1 Walk anywhere, stop on signal.	
	2 Skip anywhere.	
	3 Walk UP TO another child and stand close to him or her with your fingers touching and stretched high.	3 Remind them of Session 9.
Floor Work	1 Walk along a NARROW line on the floor.	1 Use floor boards or pretend there is a line.
	2 Slide along a NARROW line on the floor.	
	3 Travel on hands and feet. Have your hands and feet WIDE apart.	3 Select one or two examples for the rest of the class to watch and try out. Discuss with the children what they have seen.

	Content	Teaching points
Apparatus Activities	See notes on page 63; include the climbing frame	
	1 Find WIDE places where you move on the apparatus.	1 Show the children a wide piece of apparatus and a narrow piece of apparatus at first.
	2 Find NARROW places where you can move on the apparatus.	
	3 Choose whether you travel on WIDE or NARROW surfaces on the apparatus.	3 Circulate and ask individual children whether they have chosen a wide or narrow surface to travel on.
	4 Put the apparatus away.	
Calming Activity	Walk along a narrow line, then stand still.	

YEAR 1

Autumn Term ASSESSMENT AND CONSOLIDATION SESSION

The teacher needs to assess whether the children are by now fully aware of the range of actions which they can perform, together with an awareness of ways in which the space around them can be used.

They ought to be able to lift benches, box tops, low agility tables and mats safely into position.

This session can be used to make good any noted weaknesses and repeat any activity which the children found particularly enjoyable.

YEAR 1

APPARATUS Spring Term

The apparatus which the children learnt to put out last term will again be used this term, *ie.* benches, low agility/movement tables, box tops, and other low apparatus with large surfaces.

The lay-out of the apparatus can vary but should not be changed too frequently.

The children should be shown how to put out the climbing frame, if they have not already done so, providing it is easily handled by small children.

Planks can be inclined onto stools, movement tables and bar boxes etc. to provide sloping surfaces.

See notes at the beginning of the Autumn term about organizing the children on the apparatus.

YEAR 1

Spring Term Session 1: BEING AWARE OF PARTS OF THE BODY
Touching the floor with hands and feet

	Content	Teaching points
Warming Up	1 Walk anywhere on tip-toes.	
	2 Run lightly in and out of each other.	
	3 Stand on tip-toes and stretch hands high.	
Floor Work	1 Touch the floor with different parts of your feet.	1 *Eg.* heels, insteps etc.
	2 Tap the floor with different parts of your hands. Count how many parts you can find.	
	3 Make up a phrase of tapping the floor with different parts of your feet.	3 Select an example to show the class. Discuss with the children what is meant by a movement phrase.
	4 Make up a phrase of tapping the floor with different parts of your hands.	

	Content	Teaching points
Apparatus Activities	See notes on page 85.	
	1 When you use the apparatus find places where you can have part of your body on the apparatus and touch the floor with your hands.	1 Circulate and help the children to answer the task.
	2 Start away from the apparatus on a magic spot. Travel up to the apparatus touching the floor lightly with different parts of your feet. Move on the apparatus any way you like, and travel back to your magic spot with light bouncy jumps.	2 Build up the sequence gradually. Select an example for the class to watch. Discuss with the children what they have seen.
	3 Put the apparatus away.	
Calming Activity	Sit and tap your feet lightly on the floor. Stand up quietly.	

YEAR 1

Spring Term Session 2: BEING AWARE OF PARTS OF THE BODY
Touching the floor with different parts

	Content	Teaching points
Warming Up	1 Walk anywhere on your heels.	1 Keep the activity short.
	2 Run in and out of each other on your toes.	
	3 Sit down and stretch your arms and legs out.	
Floor Work	1 Whilst standing, can you lean over and touch the floor lightly with your head?	
	2 Touch the floor lightly with one elbow and then the other elbow.	
	3 Find other parts of your body to tap lightly on the floor.	3 Select a few examples for the class to watch. Discuss with the children what they have seen.
	4 Make up a phrase of tapping the floor with different parts of your body.	4 Select one example for the class to watch. Discuss with the children what they have seen.

	Content	Teaching points
Apparatus Activities	See notes on page 85.	
	1 When you use the apparatus find places where you can have part of your body on the apparatus and touch the floor with another part.	
	2 Start away from the apparatus on a magic spot. Touch the floor lightly with one part of your body, walk up to the apparatus, move on it how you like, then travel back to your magic spot with light bouncy jumps.	2 Build up the sequence gradually with the children.
	3 Put the apparatus away.	
Calming Activity	Repeat the tapping phrase you made up earlier in the lesson, stand up quietly.	

YEAR 1

Spring Term Session 3: BEING AWARE OF PARTS OF THE BODY
Travelling on hands and feet

	Content	Teaching points
Warming Up	1 Stand in a space and stretch out your arms and one leg.	
	2 Stand on one leg and stretch out the other leg.	
	3 Circle your arms backwards.	3 Slowly, try to get arms close to the ears.
	4 Run lightly anywhere on tip-toes.	
Floor Work	1 Find as many ways as you can of travelling along on your feet.	
	2 Find as many ways as you can of travelling along on your hands and feet.	2 Select a few examples for the class to watch and then try to copy. Discuss with the children all the possibilities.

	Content	Teaching points
Apparatus Activities	See notes on page 85.	
	1 How many different ways can you find of travelling along using your hands and feet?	1 Circulate and verbalize the children's responses.
	2 Start away from the apparatus on a magic spot. Travel up to the apparatus on your hands and feet, move on the apparatus any way you like, travel back to your magic spot on your hands and feet.	2 Select an example for the rest of the class to watch. Discuss with the children what they saw.
	3 Put the apparatus away.	
Calming Activity	Lie down on your side, stretch your arms and legs. Stand up quietly.	

YEAR 1

Spring Term Session 4: BEING AWARE OF PARTS OF THE BODY
Travelling on hands and feet – continued.

	Content	Teaching points
Warming Up	1 Walk anywhere on the toes of one foot and the heels of the other.	1 Demonstrate first.
	2 Run lightly anywhere taking big steps.	
	3 Stand and stretch your arms up high.	3 Circulate and encourage the children to stretch fully.
Floor Work	1 Try to remember all the ways of travelling on your feet.	1 *Eg*. hop, skip, run, walk tip-toes etc.
	2 Find as many ways as you can of travelling on two hands and one foot.	
	3 Find as many ways of travelling as you can on one hand and two feet.	
	4 Can you travel on one hand and one foot?	

Content	Teaching points
5 Make up a phrase of travelling on your hands and feet.	5 Select a good phrase for the class to watch. Discuss with the children what is good about it.

Apparatus Activities

See notes on page 85.

Content	Teaching points
1 How many different ways can you travel on your apparatus using two hands and one foot?	1 Circulate and help where necessary.
2 How many different ways can you travel on your apparatus using one hand and two feet?	
3 Can you travel on your apparatus using only one hand and one foot?	
4 Start away from your apparatus on a magic spot. Travel up to your apparatus on one hand and two feet, move on it any way you like, travel back to your magic spot on two hands and one foot.	4 Build up gradually. Select an example for the class to watch. Discuss with the children different ways hands and feet can be used.
5 Put the apparatus away.	

Calming Activity

Stand on one foot, try to keep still.
Stand on the other foot, stand still on both feet.

YEAR 1

Spring Term Session 5: BEING AWARE OF PARTS OF THE BODY
Travelling on backs, tummies, knees and elbows

	Content	Teaching points
Warming Up	1 Walk in and out of each other. On signal, stop and tuck up small.	
	2 Jump lightly in and out of each other, with your feet together.	2 Slight 'give' in the knees on take-off and landing.
Floor Work	1 Get the mats out.	1 Organize handling the mats, put in spaces all over the floor.
	2 Find a way of sliding on your back.	2 Sliding can take place on the floor or mats if they are slippery.
	3 Can you slide along on your tummy?	3 Organize the children so they take turns on the mats.
	4 Find a way of crossing the mat on your knees and elbows.	
	5 Can you cross the mat using one knee and two elbows?	

	Content	Teaching points
	6 Can you cross the mat using only one knee and one elbow?	
	7 Roll sideways across the mat tucked up small.	
	8 Roll sideways across the mat stretched out.	
Apparatus Activities	See notes on page 85; move the mats.	
	1 How many different parts of your body can you use whilst travelling on your apparatus?	1 Circulate and highlight the different parts of the body, *eg.* 'Jane is going along on her tummy'.
	2 Start away from your apparatus on a magic spot. Slide up to the apparatus on your tummy, move on it any way you like, get down carefully and roll sideways across the mat.	2 Select an example for the class to watch. Discuss with the children how the task has been attempted.
	3 Put the apparatus away.	
Calming Activity	Lie down on your back, turn over onto your tummy, kneel on your knees then stand quietly on your feet. Then: Stand up.	

YEAR 1

Spring Term Session 6:

HOLDING THE BODY STILL ON DIFFERENT PARTS
Keeping still whilst on hands and feet (Introduction to balancing activities)

	Content	Teaching points
Warming Up	1 Stand on one leg.	
	2 Walk anywhere, on signal stand on one leg.	2 Tell the children to focus their eyes on something – this will help them to keep their balance.
Floor Work	1 Put your hands and feet on the floor, can you keep still?	General points – Hands flat on floor, stretch body and try to get tension throughout the body.
	2 Put two hands and one foot on the floor, can you keep still?	
	3 Put one hand and two feet on the floor, can you keep still?	
	4 Put one hand and one foot on the floor, can you keep still?	

	Content	Teaching points
	5 Find other ways of keeping still using your hands and feet in some way?	5 Let the children show each other some of the ways they have found.
Apparatus Activities	See notes on page 85.	
	1 Find places on your apparatus where you can keep still.	1 Check that the children do not stay still for too long.
	2 Can you keep still with your weight on your hands and feet?	2 Where possible tell the children to grip the apparatus with their hands.
	3 Find places on your apparatus where you can keep still on two hands and one foot, or two feet and one hand.	
	4 Start away from your apparatus on a magic spot. Travel up to the apparatus, find somewhere on it to keep still using your hands and feet, travel back to your magic spot using bouncy jumps.	4 Select a good example for the class to watch. Discuss with the children what they saw.
	5 Put the apparatus away.	
Calming Activity	Stand on one leg and count up to five. Then: Stand on both feet.	

YEAR 1

Spring Term Session 7: HOLDING THE BODY STILL ON DIFFERENT PARTS Keeping still on knees and elbows, backs and tummies

	Content	Teaching points
Warming Up	1 Run lightly anywhere, 'freeze' on signal.	1 *ie.* hold a position when you say, 'and . . . freeze'.
	2 Run lightly anywhere, 'freeze' on one foot on signal.	2 Focus the eyes to maintain balance.
	3 Do bouncy jumps in and out of each other.	3 Feet together, slight 'give' in the knees on take-off and landing.
Floor Work	1 Practise some of the ways of keeping still on your hands and feet.	1 Try to get good tension through the body by stretching. Remind them of previous session.
	2 Find other parts of your body to keep still on.	2 Look at some examples. Get the children to tell you what parts have been used.
	3 Can you keep still on your knees and elbows?	3 Keep activity short.
	4 Can you keep still on your backs?	4 Head, arms and legs off the floor. Remember to stretch.

	Content	Teaching points
	5 Can you keep still on your tummies?	5 Head, chest and legs off the floor, arch the back.
Apparatus Activities	See notes on page 85.	
	1 Find places where you can keep still on interesting parts of your body.	1 If the children find it difficult to stay still suggest they count up to five before moving on.
	2 Find a place where you can keep still on one part of your body, then find another place where you can be still on a different part.	2 Circulate and encourage the children to think of different parts of the body.
	3 Start away from your apparatus on a magic spot, keep still on that spot on part of your body, travel up to your apparatus in a interesting way, keep still on it using knees and elbows, or backs or tummies.. Slide back to your magic spot.	3 Build the sequence up gradually by asking all the children to keep still on their magic spots first. Select an example for the class to watch. Encourage the children to tell you about what they saw.
	4 Put the apparatus away.	
Calming Activity	Lie down on your back. Then: Stand up.	

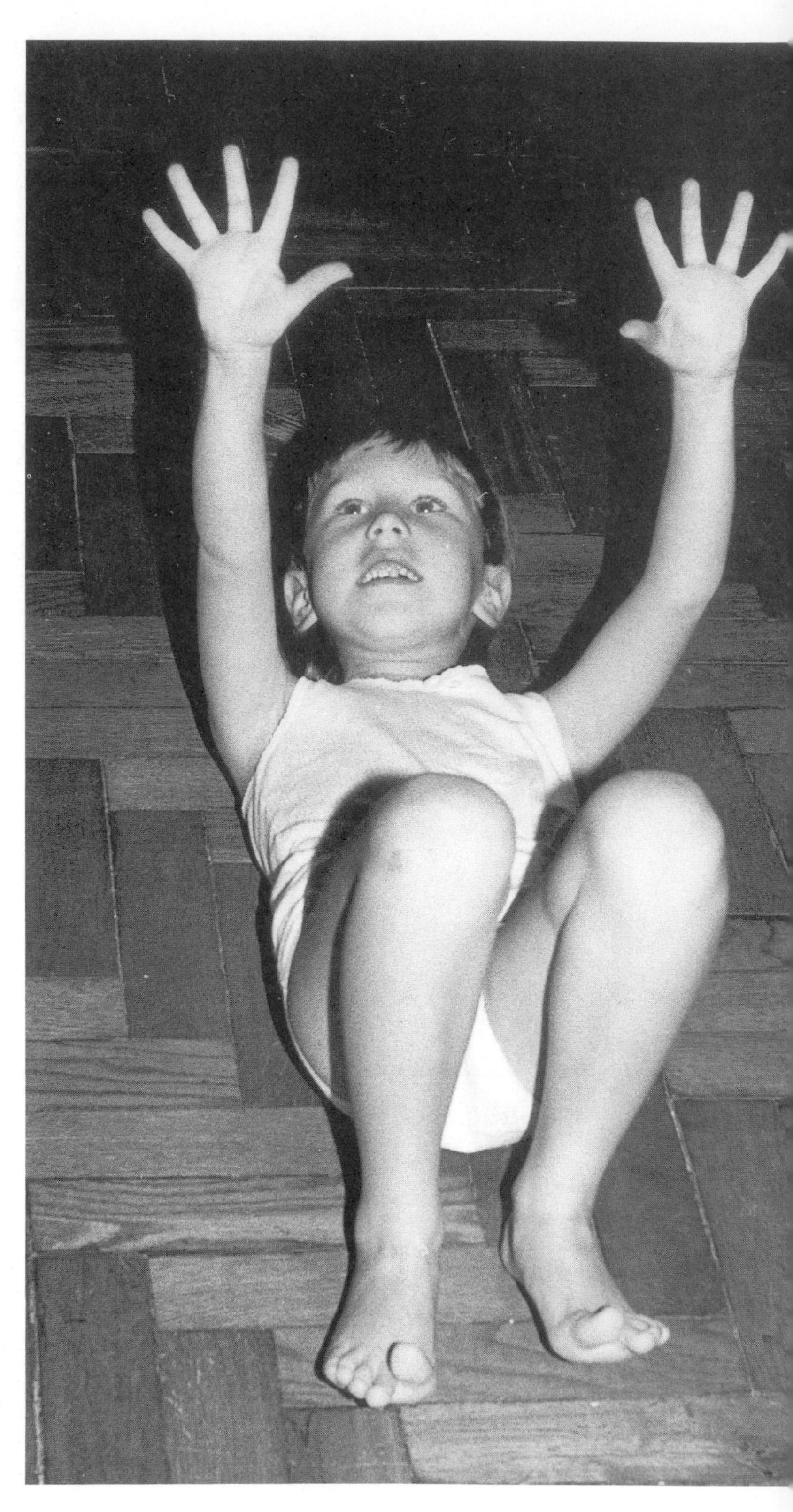

Finding parts of your body to keep still on (Spring term, Session 7).

Find places where you can be still on your apparatus. Tuck your body up as much as possible. (Spring term, Session 8).

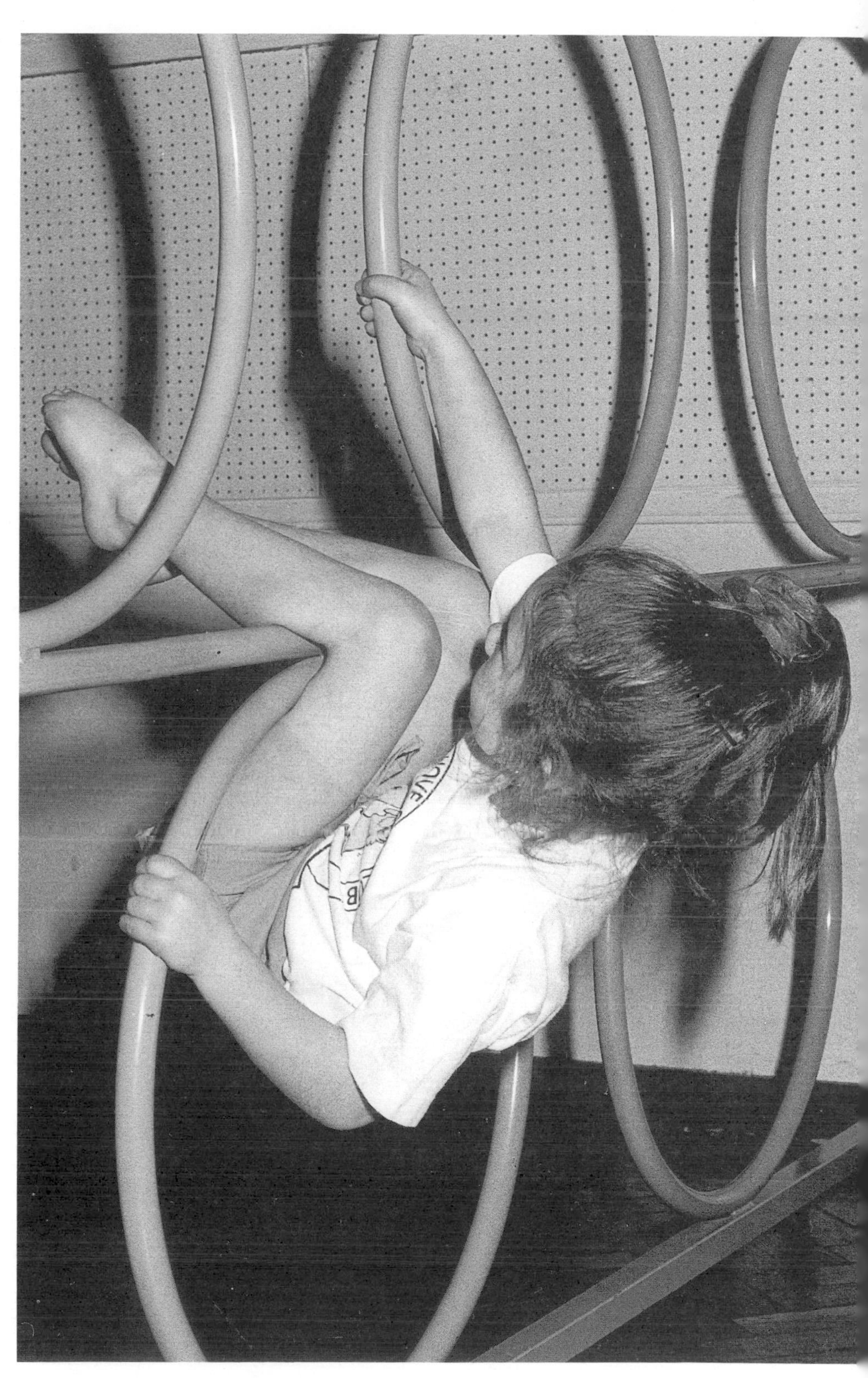

YEAR 1

Spring Term Session 8: STRETCHING OUT AND TUCKING UP
Holding stretched and tucked positions

	Content	Teaching points
Warming Up	1 Walk anywhere stretching out your legs.	1 Encourage a good stretch of one leg and then the other.
	2 Run lightly in and out of each other, stop on signal and stretch your arms out.	2 Circulate and make sure they all stretch their arms as much as possible.
Floor Work	1 Whilst on your hands and feet stretch your body as much as possible.	1 Stretch all the body.
	2 Whilst on your hands and feet tuck your body up as much as possible.	2 Look at a good stretched position and a good tucked position. Discuss the difference with the children.
	3 Choose part of your body to be still on, then stretch all the other parts out as much as possible.	
	4 Choose other parts to be still on. Tuck the rest of your body up as much as possible.	

	Content	Teaching points
Apparatus Activities	See notes on page 85.	
	1 Find places where you can be still on your apparatus, stretch your body out as much as possible.	1 Circulate and make suggestions.
	2 Find places where you can be still on your apparatus. Tuck your body up as much as possible.	2 Check the children tuck up as small as they can.
	3 Choose whether you are stretched or tucked when you are still on the apparatus.	3 Look at one or two examples. Get the children to identify tucked and stretched positions.
	4 Start away from the apparatus on a magic spot. Stretch out on that spot in an interesting way. Travel up to your apparatus, find where you can be stretched or tucked up on it, do bouncy jumps back to your magic spot.	
Calming Activity	Lie on your back and stretch out. Then: Stand up.	

YEAR 1

Spring Term Session 9: STRETCHING OUT AND TUCKING UP
Moving in stretched out and tucked up positions

	Content	Teaching points
Warming Up	1 Walk anywhere, stop on signal, stretch arms up in the air.	
	2 Run lightly in and out of each other.	
	3 Skip lightly in and out of each other, stop on signal and tuck up small.	
Floor Work	1 Spring up into the air. Stretch your body whilst in the air.	1 Slight 'give' in the knees on take-off and landing.
	2 Travel on hands and feet, stretch arms and legs as you go along.	
	3 Travel on hands and feet, keeping your body tucked up.	

Content	Teaching points
4 Find other ways of travelling. Choose whether you are stretched out or tucked up as you go along.	4 Look at a few examples. Ask the children 'Who is really stretched?' 'Who is very tucked up small?'

Apparatus Activities

See notes on page 85.

Content	Teaching points
1 Travel on hands and feet on the apparatus stretching out as you go.	1 Circulate and ensure the children stretch to the limit.
2 Travel on hands and feet on the apparatus tucking up as you go.	2 Encourage tucking up as tightly as possible.
3 Travel on other parts of the body either stretching out or tucking up as you go.	
4 Start away from your apparatus on a magic spot, travel up to your apparatus stretched out, move on it tucked up, travel back to your magic spot stretched out.	4 Look at a good example. Discuss with the children how the task has been attempted.
5 Put the apparatus away.	

Calming Activity

In a space tuck up small. Gradually stretch out as the teacher counts up to ten. Stand up tall.

YEAR 1

Spring Term Session 10: STRETCHING OUT AND TUCKING UP
Stretching out and tucking up whilst travelling

	Content	Teaching points
Warming Up	1 Walk anywhere, on signal stop and stretch arms and legs.	1 The weight need not be on the feet in order to stretch.
	2 Run lightly in and out of each other, on signal tuck up small.	2 Circulate and check they are tucked up as small as possible.
Floor Work	1 Start on your feet tucked up. Jump high in the air, tuck up small as you land.	1 See 'Jack-in-a-box' on page 69.
	2 Start on your back tucked up. Roll over sideways stretching out as you roll.	
	3 Start on your tummy stretched out. Roll over sideways, tucking up small as you roll.	
	4 Sit tucked up. Spin round and stretch out as you spin.	

	Content	Teaching points
Apparatus Activities	See notes on page 85.	
	1 Try to stretch out and then tuck up as you travel on the apparatus.	1 Circulate and encourage stretching and tucking as they travel.
	2 Find where you can stretch out on the apparatus then try to tuck up small.	
	3 Find places where you can jump off the apparatus, stretching out as you jump.	3 Watch landings.
	4 Start away from the apparatus on a magic spot. Do bouncy jumps up to the apparatus, change from stretching out to tucking up as you travel on your apparatus. Do stretched jumps back to your magic spot.	4 Watch landings.
	5 Put the apparatus away.	
Calming Activity	Lie down on your side in a tucked position. Turn over onto your back stretching out as you turn. Then: Stand up.	

YEAR 1

Spring Term ASSESSMENT AND CONSOLIDATION SESSION

The children by now should:

1 Have consolidated all that they learnt in the Reception year.

2 Be more knowledgeable about the range of actions the body can do and the part they have to play in Gymnastic-like activity.

3 Have begun to develop an understanding about how to perform specific actions in a variety of situations.

4 Have developed an awareness of the role different parts of the body have to play in movement.

5 Have increased their knowledge and understanding of how the space surrounding the body can be used to good advantage.

6 Be able to lift benches, box tops, low agility/movement tables, stools, inclined planks, the climbing frame and mats into position.

This session can be used to make good any noted weaknesses and repeat any activity which the children found particularly enjoyable.

For your notes and comments:

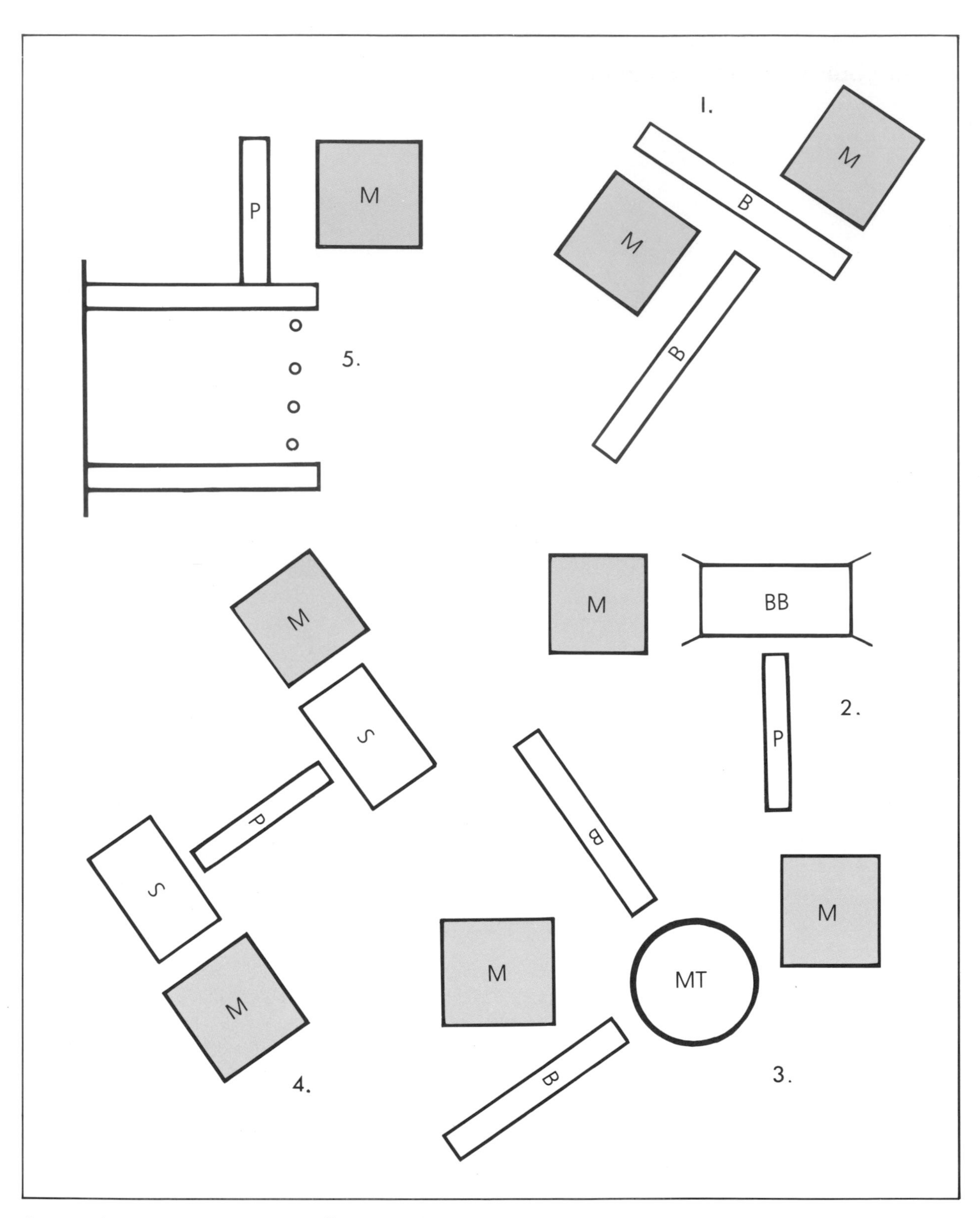

A sample apparatus pattern for Year 2.

YEAR 2: INTRODUCTION

APPARATUS Autumn and Spring Terms

The children by now should be able to move all the apparatus and set it in position safely and responsively. If, however, some of it is too heavy then a compromise has to be reached, *i.e.* the children put out some of it and the rest is set out beforehand by adults, or the apparatus work takes place in another lesson.

As in Year 1 the children should be in five or six groups and allocated a 'station' at which to start work. This year they will be expected to stay at each 'station' for much longer, selecting, practising and perfecting a sequence of movements which can, if appropriate, be performed for the rest of the class.

In the Autumn term for sessions 1 to 6 the apparatus should be set out in such a way as to provide opportunities for the children to travel along it, therefore benches, inclined planks and balance bars etc. will be needed.

For sessions 7 to 10 each 'station' should consist of a combination of apparatus, preferably not set out in a straight line.

In the Spring term different arrangements can be used, but the layout should not be altered too frequently. One layout should last for at least four lessons. Large surfaces and benches are particularly useful.

YEAR 2

Autumn Term Session 1: USING THE ACTIONS
Walk, run and stop

	Content	Teaching points
Warming Up	1 Walk, quietly anywhere.	1 Encourage walking all over the floor, not just round the room.
	2 Stand and circle arms.	2 Slowly backwards, close to the ears.
	3 Stretch one leg out and then the other.	
Floor Work	1 Use a walking action to get in and out of each other.	1 Emphasize the walking in and out.
	2 Use a running action to get in and out of each other.	2 Encourage a good running action, high knee lift, bent arms.
	3 Use a running action to travel into a space, stop and count up to three, then run into a new space.	
	4 Start on a magic spot, use a running action to go round the room and back to your magic spot.	

	Content	Teaching points
	5 Do ten bouncy jumps on your magic spot. Stop and then do five more.	5 'Give' slightly in the knees on take-off and landing.
Apparatus Activities	See introduction on page 111.	
	1 Use a running action to go in and out of your apparatus without touching it.	
	2 Use a walking action to get along the apparatus.	2 Where possible, *eg*. benches.
	3 Start away from your apparatus on a magic spot. Use a running action to travel up to the apparatus, use a walking action to take you along the apparatus, travel back to your magic spot a different way.	3 Select a few examples for the rest of the class to watch. Discuss with the children the way the actions are used.
	4 Put the apparatus away.	
Calming Activity	Use a walking action to find your magic spot. Stand still on your magic spot.	

YEAR 2

Autumn Term Session 2: **USING THE ACTIONS**
Slide, spin, push, pull

	Content	Teaching points
Warming Up	1 Use a walking action to travel round the room.	
	2 Use a running action to dodge and swerve.	2 Discuss with the children how to do this, *ie,* take small steps, turn the shoulders, lean etc.
	3 Stand and stretch one leg out in front of you, then the other.	
Floor Work	1 Use a sliding action to travel along the floor.	1 On different parts of the body, backs, tummies, seats.
	2 Use a spinning action to turn round and round.	
	3 Use a pushing action to jump high in the air.	3 Push with the feet, bend knees on take-off and landing.
	4 Use a pulling action to slide on your tummy.	4 *ie.* hands on the floor.

	Content	Teaching points
Apparatus Activities	As for session 1 on page 112.	
	1 Find places on your apparatus where you can use a sliding action to get along.	1 Circulate and encourage sliding in different ways.
	2 Find places where you can push yourself along or pull yourself up.	2 Select one or two examples for the class to watch. Discuss with the children how the actions were being used.
	3 Start away from your apparatus on a magic spot. Use a spinning action to turn round and round on the spot. Then use a walking action to get up to your apparatus. Find ways of using pushing or pulling actions on your apparatus. Travel back to your magic spot in some way.	3 Build up the sequence gradually.
Calming Activity	Sit in a space, spin round and round. Stand up quietly.	

YEAR 2

Autumn Term Session 3: **USING THE ACTIONS**
Jumping, hopping and skipping (without ropes)

	Content	Teaching points
Warming Up	1 Walk quietly in and out of each other.	
	2 Use a running action to dodge and swerve in and out of each other.	
	3 Stand and stretch your arms in the air.	
Floor Work	1 Use bouncy jumps to travel all over the floor.	1 Bend knees slightly on take-off and landing.
	2 Use skipping to go round the room.	
	3 Start at one end of the room. Use hopping to get to the other end.	3 This is not a race, let some go at a time.
	4 Make up a phrase using jumping skipping and hopping.	4 Keep simple. Select a good example for the rest to copy.

	Content	Teaching points
Apparatus Activities	As for session 1 on page 112.	
	1 As you use the apparatus find somewhere where you can use a hop to go along.	
	2 As you use the apparatus find somewhere you can use a skipping action to go along.	2 This may not be possible at all stations. If not, the children can skip back to the start.
	3 Find somewhere where you can use a jump to get on, off or over a piece of apparatus.	
	4 Start on a magic spot. Skip up to your apparatus move on it how you like, jump off and hop back to your magic spot.	4 Select an example for the rest of the class to watch. Discuss with the children how the actions were used.
	5 Put the apparatus away.	
Calming Activity	Walk quietly in and out of each other till you find a space. Stand still in that space.	

YEAR 2

Autumn Term Session 4: USING THE ACTIONS With rotation (turning)

	Content	Teaching points
Warming Up	1 Hop in and out of each other.	
	2 Skip round the room.	
	3 Stand and circle your arms.	3 Backwards, slowly, close to ears.
Floor Work	Mats will be needed	
	1 Walk, on signal turn and walk somewhere else.	1 Turn sharply.
	2 Run, stop on signal, turn and run somewhere else.	
	3 Sit and spin round and round.	
	4 On your hands and feet, with back to the ceiling find a way of turning over.	4 Only hands and feet to touch the floor.

Content	Teaching points
5 On a mat use a rolling action to travel sideways, tucked up or stretched out.	5 Get the mats out first.
6 On a mat do a forward roll to get along it.	6 See **Specific Skills Guide.**

Apparatus Work

As for session 1 on page 112.

Content	Teaching points
1 Find places where you can turn round on your apparatus.	
2 Find places where you can turn over on your apparatus.	2 If necessary discuss with the children the difference between turning over and round.
3 Use your apparatus any way you like. Jump off and land on a mat. Use a rolling action to travel along the mat.	
4 Start away from the apparatus on a magic spot, facing away from it. Travel up to it in some way. Turn round on it, use a rolling action to travel across your mat.	
5 Put the apparatus away.	

Calming Activity

Sit and spin round and round.
Stand up quietly.

YEAR 2

Autumn Term Session 5: USING THE ACTIONS To travel quickly or slowly

	Content	Teaching points
Warming Up	1 Walk quietly in and out of each other.	
	2 Using a light run swerve and dodge in and out of each other.	2 Good use of feet to swerve and dodge.
	3 Hop, on signal turn and hop in another direction.	3 Say, 'and . . . turn'.
Floor Work	1 Run anti-clockwise round the room. Start slowly and gradually get quicker. Slow down on signal.	1 Explain what to do first.
	2 Use fast bouncy jumps to get you all over the room.	2 Try not to lose the quality of the jumps.
	3 Travel slowly on your hands and feet into a new space.	
	4 Slide slowly, then spin round quickly.	

Content	Teaching points
5 On a mat, roll sideways slowly.	5 Get the mats out first.
6 On a mat, roll forwards slowly.	6 See **Specific Skills Guide.**

Apparatus Activities

As for session 1 on page 112.

Content	Teaching points
1 Find places where you can travel slowly on your apparatus.	1 Circulate and make sure they do not travel too slowly.
2 Find places where you can travel quickly and SAFELY on your apparatus.	
3 Start away from your apparatus on a magic spot. Travel up to your apparatus slowly, move on it how you like, get off and run quickly back to your magic spot.	3 Select one or two examples for the rest of the class to watch. Discuss with the children what they saw.

Calming Activity

Tuck up small in a space, gradually stretch out as far as possible. Tuck up small in space, stretch out quickly. Stand tall.

YEAR 2

Autumn Term Session 6: USING THE ACTIONS To travel strongly or lightly

	Content	Teaching points
Warming Up	1 Use a hopping action to get in and out of each other.	
	2 Use a skipping action to get round the room.	
	3 Stand and stretch one leg out and then the other.	
Floor Work	1 Use a lot of strength to spring high in the air.	1 Use arms to help, bend knees slightly on take-off and landing.
	2 Use your feet in a variety of ways to travel lightly all over the floor.	2 Look at a few examples. Discuss ways of using feet.
	3 Lie on your tummy, push strongly with your hands to do a sliding action.	
	4 Find other ways of pushing or pulling strongly with your hands to do a sliding action.	

	Content	Teaching points
Apparatus Activities	As for session 1 on page 112.	
	1 Find places where you need a lot of strength to climb, pull, hang etc. on your apparatus.	
	2 Start away from your apparatus on a magic spot. Travel lightly on your feet in an interesting way up to your apparatus. Find somewhere on your apparatus where you can be strong. Walk lightly on tip-toes back to your magic spot.	2 Build up gradually.
	3 Put your apparatus away.	
Calming Activity	Do five big strong jumps on the spot. Stretch up lightly. Stand tall.	

YEAR 2

Autumn Term Session 7: **USING THE SPACE**
Introduction to going in different directions

	Content	Teaching points
Warming Up	1 Walk anywhere. Stop on signal.	
	2 Walk anywhere, on signal turn and walk somewhere else.	
	3 Run lightly round the room, anti-clockwise.	
Floor Work	1 Do bouncy jumps anywhere.	
	2 Can you do bouncy jumps and go backwards?	2 Tell the children to look over their shoulders to see where they are going.
	3 Can you do bouncy jumps and go sideways?	
	4 Choose different ways of travelling. Can you go backwards?	4 Discuss different ways to choose from. Select a few examples for the children to try to copy.

	Content	Teaching points
	5 Choose other ways of travelling. Can you go sideways?	
	6 Find ways of going up and down on the spot.	
Apparatus Activities	Choose a different layout.	
	1 Find places where you can go sideways on your apparatus.	
	2 Find places where you can go backwards on your apparatus.	2 This does not mean they have to go bckwards all the time.
	3 Find places where you can go up and down on your apparatus.	
	4 Choose different directions to go on your apparatus.	4 Circulate and verbalize the responses, *Eg*. 'Mary is sliding backwards down the plank'.
	5 Start away from your apparatus on a magic spot. Travel up to your apparatus forwards, travel on it any way you like. Go back to your magic spot sideways.	
	6 Put the apparatus away.	
Calming Activity	Walk quietly in and out of each other. Choose whether you go forwards, backwards or sideways. Then: Stand still.	

YEAR 2

Autumn Term Session 8: USING THE SPACE — Going forwards and backwards

	Content	Teaching points
Warming Up	1 Walk anywhere using all the space.	
	2 Walk backwards using all the space.	2 Look over your shoulder to see where you are going.
	3 Do bouncy jumps on the spot.	
Floor Work	1 Find a variety of ways of going forwards on your feet.	1 Discuss possibilities first.
	2 Do the same but try to go backwards.	
	3 Find ways of travelling on your hands and feet. Go forwards and then go backwards.	3 Select one or two examples for the rest of the class to watch and try to copy.
	4 Travel on other parts of your body. Go forwards and then go backwards.	
	5 Roll forwards on a mat.	5 Get the mats out first. See **Specific Skills Guide.**

	Content	Teaching points
Apparatus Activities	As for session 7 on page 125.	
	1 Find places on your apparatus where you can go forwards.	1 Circulate and make suggestions to extend the children.
	2 Find places on your apparatus where you can go backwards.	
	3 On your apparatus sometimes go forwards and sometimes go backwards.	
	4 Start away from your apparatus on a magic spot. Travel backwards up to your apparatus travel forwards on it, roll forwards on the mat.	4 Select one or two examples for the rest of the children to watch. Discuss with the children, 'Where did (s)he go forwards and where backwards. What actions did (s)he do?'
	5 Put the apparatus away.	
Calming Activity	Walk quietly in and out of each other. Sometimes walk forwards and sometimes walk backwards. Lie down in a space. Then: Stand up.	

YEAR 2

Autumn Term Session 9: USING THE SPACE Going up and down

	Content	Teaching points
Warming Up	1 Stand in a space and stretch your arms up in the air.	
	2 Stand in a space. Stretch one leg out and then the other.	
	3 Walk quickly anywhere, going either forwards or backwards.	
	4 Can you hop backwards?	4 Watch spacing. Look over your shoulder to see where you are going.
Floor Work	1 Start low near the floor and spring high, bend your knees when you land.	1 Slight 'give' in the knees on take-off and landing.
	2 On your hands and feet facing the floor, raise your hips then lower them again, do this several times.	

	Content	Teaching points
	3 Find ways of travelling and going up and down at the same time.	3 Discuss ways of travelling with the children first to get ideas.
Apparatus Activities	As for session 7 on page 125.	
	1 Find places on your apparatus where you can go up and down.	1 Circulate and verbalize the responses.
	2 Find places on your apparatus where you can travel along and go up and down at the same time.	
	3 Try to go in different directions as you use the apparatus.	3 Ask the children to name the direction.
	4 Start away from your apparatus on a magic spot. Travel forwards in an interesting way up to your apparatus, move up and down on it then travel backwards to your magic spot.	4 Build up gradually. Choose a good example for the rest to watch. Discuss with the children what they saw.
	5 Put the apparatus away.	
Calming Activity	Stand in a space, crouch down, stretch up high and then crouch down again. Do this ten times.	The heels should come off the floor when crouched down.
	Stand quietly.	

YEAR 2

Autumn Term Session 10: **USING THE SPACE Going sideways**

	Content	Teaching points
Warming Up	1 Walk in and out of each other.	
	2 Run lightly round the room, anti-clockwise.	
	3 Stand and circle your arms backwards.	
Floor Work	1 Can you step sideways across the room?	1 Left and right sides of the body can lead.
	2 Using your feet, find different ways of going sideways.	
	3 Find different ways of travelling sideways on your hands and feet.	
	4 Can you travel sideways on any other part of your body?	

Content	Teaching points
5 Make up a phrase of movements, include going in different directions.	5 Select a few examples for the class to watch. Discuss with the children what they have seen.

Apparatus Activities

As for session 7 on page 125.

Content	Teaching points
1 Find places where you can move sideways on your apparatus.	1 This does not mean they have to move sideways all the time.
2 Travel in different directions on your apparatus.	2 Circulate and make suggestions.
3 Start away from your apparatus on a magic spot. Find an interesting way to travel forwards up to your apparatus, move sideways on it, travel backwards to your magic spot again.	
4 Put your apparatus away.	

Calming Activity

1 Stand in a space with your feet apart. Rock gently from side to side.

2 Find ways of rocking from side to side on other parts of your body.

3 Stand tall.

YEAR 2

Autumn Term

ASSESSMENT AND CONSOLIDATION SESSION.

By now the children should be able to:

1 Use the basic actions in a variety of ways.

2 Do a forward roll.

3 Make up simple movement phrases which they can remember and perform to the rest of the class.

4 Have been introduced to the units of rotation, travelling, balance and springing (jumping) and landing which go to make up the units in Key Stage 2.

5 Understand that movements can be performed quickly or slowly, strongly or lightly and in different directions.

6 Handle all the apparatus safely (providing it is designed to be handled by Infants).

This session can be used to make good any noted weaknesses and repeat any activity which the children found particularly enjoyable.

For your notes and comments

YEAR 2

Spring Term Session 1: USING PARTS OF THE BODY
To take weight whilst moving

	Content	Teaching points
Warming Up	1 Walk anywhere on tip-toes.	
	2 Walk anywhere on your heels.	2 Keep activity short.
	3 Run lightly in and out of each other using a good arm action.	3 *ie.* pumping action with bent arms, fists slightly clenched.
Floor Work	1 Use your feet in different ways to go along.	1 Make suggestions, and get ideas from the children.
	2 Find different ways of using your hands and feet to go along.	2 Select a few for the class to watch. Discuss what parts of the body are used.
	3 Can you go along on other parts of your body?	

	Content	Teaching points
Apparatus Activities	Choose a new layout.	
	1 Use your hands and feet to travel in as many ways as you can.	1 Circulate and verbalize the responses.
	2 Use other parts of your body to travel on your apparatus.	
	3 Start away from your apparatus on a magic spot. Use your feet and hands to travel up to it, move on it how you like, travel back to your magic spot on your feet in an interesting way.	3 Build up gradualiy. Choose a good example for the class to watch. Get the children to tell you what they have seen.
Calming Activity	Sit on the floor in a space. Use your hands to spin you round. Stand up tall.	

YEAR 2

Spring Term Session 2: USING PARTS OF THE BODY To take weight whilst still

	Content	Teaching points
Warming Up	1 Run lightly in and out of each other using a good arm action.	
	2 Stand on one leg and stretch your arms up high.	2 Focus the eyes on one point to assist balance.
	3 Do four bouncy jumps on the spot. Turn to face a new direction and then do four more.	
Floor Work	1 Find a way of balancing on your hands and feet.	1 Discuss what we mean by balancing, *ie,* keeping steady on a small base. Encourage a good stretch.
	2 Can you balance using two hands and one foot?	
	3 Can you balance using one hand and two feet?	
	4 Can you balance using one hand and one foot?	

	Content	Teaching points
	5 Choose other parts to balance on.	5 Choose some examples for the class to watch and try to copy. Ask what parts are being used to balance on.
	6 Can you balance on only one part?	
Apparatus Activities	Same layout as page 135.	
	1 Use interesting parts of your body to balance on the apparatus.	1 Circulate and make suggestions.
	2 Can you balance with your hands on the floor and the rest of your body on the apparatus?	2 Make sure this is possible.
	3 Start away from the apparatus on a magic spot. Travel up to the apparatus in an interesting way, balance on it in some way, travel back to your magic spot using your feet.	3 Build up gradually. Select a good example for the rest of the class to watch. Ask what parts are being used to balance on.
Calming Activity	Find a space and stand on one leg, try to keep still whilst the teacher counts up to ten. Then: Stand on both feet.	

YEAR 2

Spring Term Session 3: **USING PARTS OF THE BODY**
To transfer weight from feet to hands (1)

	Content	Teaching points
Warming Up	1 Walk anywhere using your feet in as many ways as you can.	
	2 Hop on one foot then the other.	
	3 Do light bouncy jumps on the spot.	
	4 Find other ways of jumping.	4 Half the class watch the other half. Choose a way of jumping that is new to you and try it.
Floor Work	1 Practise bunny hops.	1 Hands flat on floor under shoulders, arms straight, jump feet up to hands. See **Specific Skills Guide.**
	2 Do bunny hops in other directions.	2 *eg.* sideways.
	3 Can you do one-handed bunny hops?	

	Content	Teaching points
	4 Can you use one hand and then the other when you do one-handed bunny hops?	
	5 Can you do bunny hops using two hands and one foot?	
	6 Find ways of going from your feet to your hands and back to your feet again.	6 Make sure weight is put on the hands. Discuss what we mean by transferring weight.
Apparatus Activities	Use benches and mats if possible.	
	1 Use your feet and hands to do bunny hops along a bench.	1 Feet can be on the floor or on the bench.
	2 Find other ways to do bunny hop-like actions along a bench.	2 Remind them of the floor work.
	3 Find ways of using your apparatus to transfer your weight from feet to hands and back to feet.	
	4 Start away from your apparatus on a magic spot. Do bunny hops up your apparatus, move on it how you like, travel back to your magic spot on hands and feet another way.	4 Build up gradually, Select one or two examples for the rest of the class to watch. Discuss how the weight is transferred.
	5 Put the apparatus away.	
Calming Activity	Lie down quietly on the floor. Listen to any sounds you can hear. Then: Stand up.	

YEAR 2

Spring Term Session 4: USING PARTS OF THE BODY
To transfer weight from feet to hands (2)

	Content	Teaching points
Warming Up	1 Run lightly round the room using a good arm action.	1 Pumping action with bent arms.
	2 Practise bunny hops.	2 Watch spacing.
Floor Work	1 Practise all the ways of doing bunny hops you can think of.	1 Remind them of previous session.
	2 Find other ways of going from feet to hands and back to feet again.	2 Keep arms straight, avoid over-balancing by moving one hand forwards.
	3 Place one hand on the floor jump your feet up to that hand then place the other hand on the floor and jump your feet up to it again.	3 Talk about cartwheels, explain about the spokes of a wheel. Refer to **Specific Skills Guide.**
	4 Place one hand on the floor, then place the other hand on the floor ahead of it, then jump your feet so they land close to the second hand.	

Content	Teaching points
5 Do this again turning round as you go.	5 Choose a child who is doing it correctly for them to watch.
6 Do this again but land one foot after the other.	6 Mini-cartwheels – legs are bent at this stage. Help children to get the sequencing right.

Apparatus Activities

Choose a new layout, using benches and large surfaces

Content	Teaching points
1 Find ways of going from feet to hands and back to feet on the apparatus.	
2 Find somewhere you can go from your feet onto one hand and back onto your feet again.	2 Feet can remain on the floor.
3 Start away from your apparatus on a magic spot. Travel up to your apparatus going from feet to hands and back to your feet again. Move on it any way you choose, travel back to your magic spot using one hand and two feet.	3 Build up gradually.
4 Put your apparatus away.	

Calming Activity

Stand up quietly.

YEAR 2

Spring Term Session 5: USING PARTS OF THE BODY To transfer weight

	Content	Teaching points
Warming Up	1 Walk anywhere going from one foot to the other.	
	2 Run lightly in and out of each other.	
	3 Practise bunny hops.	
Floor Work	1 Use different parts of your body to balance on.	1 Revise session 2.
	2 Balance on your seat, turn and then balance on your tummy. Try not to let any other part of your body touch the floor.	
	3 Use part of your body to balance on then try to balance on a different part.	3 Without altering the body position too much.
	4 Use part of your body to balance on, turn or lean over in order to balance on a different part.	4 Look at a few examples and let the children try to copy them.

	Content	Teaching points
Apparatus Activities	As for last session.	
	1 Find places where you can balance on your apparatus.	1 Circulate and suggest parts of the body to balance on.
	2 Balance on one part then transfer your weight onto another part.	
	3 Start away from your apparatus on a magic spot. Travel up to the apparatus on your hands and feet, balance on the apparatus, transfer your weight onto another part. Then travel back to your magic spot using your feet in an interesting way.	3 Build up gradually. Select a good example for the rest of thc class to watch. Discuss with the children what they have seen.
	4 Put the apparatus away.	
Calming Activity	1 Find a space. Do a shoulder balance.	1 *ie.* legs straight, stretched above head, weight on the shoulders and top part of the spine. Hands support body on waist.
	Then: Stand up.	(See page 146 photograph)

YEAR 2

Autumn Term Session 6: **USING PARTS OF THE BODY**
To jump and land with the feet either together or apart

	Content	Teaching points
Warming Up	1 Walk anywhere taking large steps.	1 Put the feet down carefully.
	2 Run in and out of each other, stop on signal with your feet apart.	
	3 Stand with your feet together. Circle your arms backwards.	3 Slowly, hands close to ears.
Floor Work	1 Practise star jumps.	1 Start with feet together, part them in the air, bring feet together on landing.
	2 Do light bouncy jumps with your feet together.	
	3 Make up a phrase to include star jumps and bouncy jumps.	3 Select a few examples for the rest of the class to watch. Discuss what makes a good movement phrase.

	Content	Teaching points
Apparatus Activities	Large surfaces to jump from.	
	1 Find places on your apparatus where you can do bouncy jumps.	1 If possible; or floor can be used as part of the apparatus.
	2 Find places where you can do star jumps.	
	3 Start away from your apparatus on a magic spot. Travel up to your apparatus doing bouncy jumps with your feet together, move on it in any way you choose, travel back to your magic spot doing star jumps.	3 Build up gradually, select an example for the class to watch. Discuss when the feet are apart and when they are together.
	4 Put your apparatus away.	
Calming Activity	Lie down on your back with your feet together. Then: Stand up	

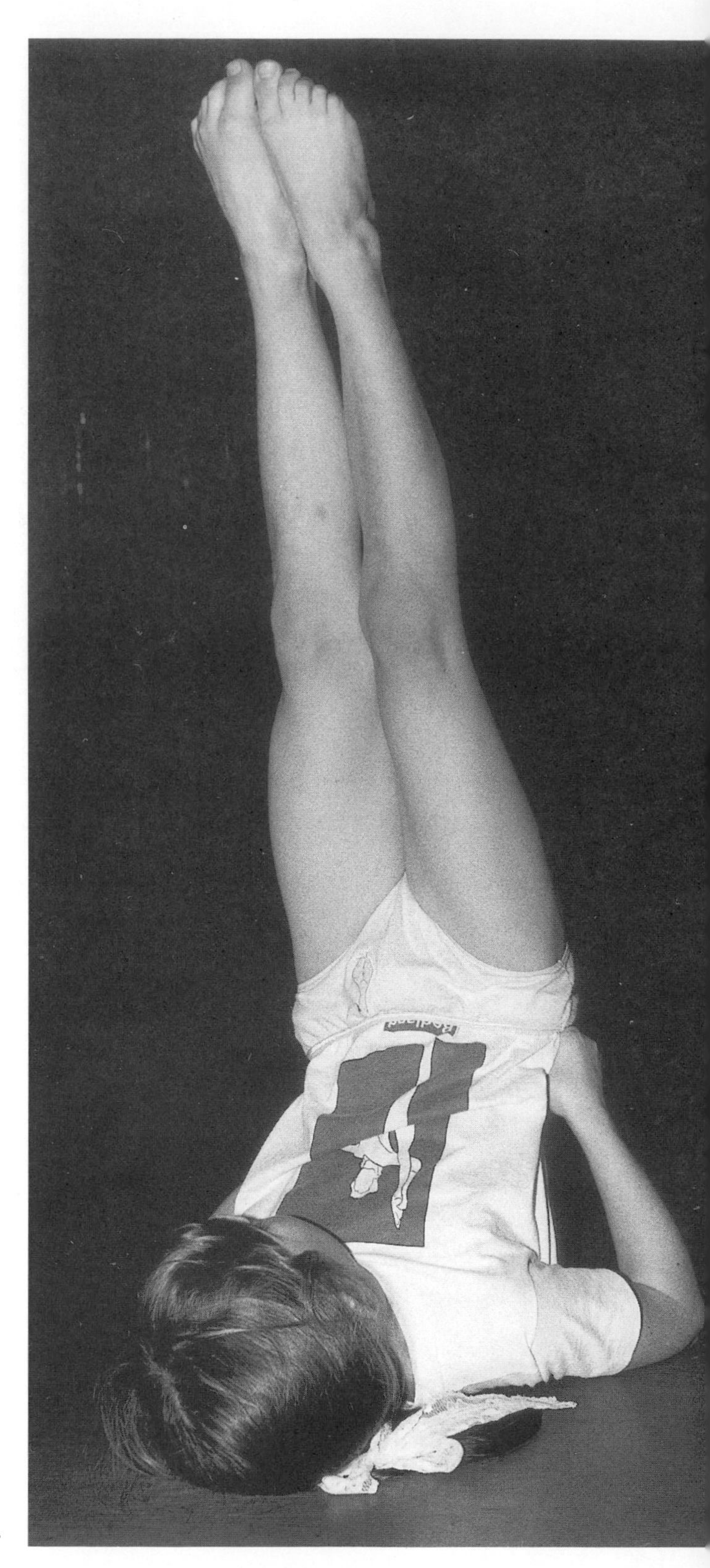

A shoulder balance (Spring term, Session 5).

On your apparatus find places where you can travel with your feet apart, (Spring term, Session7).

YEAR 2

Spring Term Session 7: USING PARTS OF THE BODY

To travel on hands and feet, with the feet either together or apart

	Content	Teaching points
Warming Up	1 Walk anywhere taking large steps.	1 Put feet down quietly.
	2 Run in and out of each other, stop on signal with feet apart and arms outstretched.	2 Explain the word 'outstretched'.
	3 Do bouncy jumps with your feet together, moving around.	
Floor Work	1 Find a way of travelling using your hands and feet. Keep your feet together as you go.	1 Discuss different ways first.
	2 Now try to travel the same way but have your feet apart.	

Content	Teaching points
3 Travel on hands and feet in different ways. Sometimes have your feet together and sometimes apart.	3 Look at some examples. Children to tell you whether the feet are together or apart.
4 Practise mini-cartwheels.	4 See session 4.

Apparatus Activities

Choose a new layout.

Content	Teaching points
1 Find places where you can travel with your feet together.	1 Circulate and make suggestions.
2 Find places where you can travel with your feet apart.	
3 Choose whether you have your feet together or apart.	
4 Start away from your apparatus on a magic spot. Travel up to your apparatus on hands and feet, move on your apparatus in any way you choose, travel back to your apparatus doing bouncy jumps. Keep your feet together as much as possible.	4 Select an example for the class to watch. Ask 'Where were the feet together and where were they apart?'
5 Put the apparatus away.	

Calming Activity

Stand quietly in a space with your feet together.

YEAR 2

Spring Term Session 8: USING PARTS OF THE BODY
To slide and roll, with the feet either together or apart

	Content	Teaching points
Warming Up	1 Walk in and out of each other.	
	2 Run into a space. Jump up and down in that space.	
	3 Practise bunny hops.	3 Watch spacing.
Floor Work	Get the mats out.	
	1 On a mat, roll sideways, tucked up, with your feet together.	1 Discourage covering the eyes.
	2 On a mat, roll sideways, stretched out, with your feet apart.	2 Fully stretched.
	3 On a mat, roll forwards with your feet together.	3 See **Specific Skills Guide.**
	4 On the floor slide with your feet together.	4 Some can slide whilst others are rolling on the mats.

	Content	Teaching points
	5 Slide with your feet apart.	
	6 Make up a phrase to include rolling and sliding. Sometimes have your feet together and sometimes apart.	
Apparatus Activities	Use the same layout.	
	1 Find places where you can slide with your feet together or apart.	1 Circulate and make suggestions.
	2 Find places where you can roll with your feet together or part.	2 Probably on a mat, some may roll on a box top, for example.
	3 Start away from your apparatus on a magic spot. Slide up to your apparatus with your feet together. Move on it any way you choose, roll on a mat with your feet apart.	3 Build up gradually. Select one or two examples for the rest to watch and comment on.
	4 Put the apparatus away.	
Calming Activity	Sit on the floor with your feet apart. Spin round and round. Stand up quietly.	

YEAR 2

Spring Term Session 9: **USING PARTS OF THE BODY To travel along straight lines**

	Content	Teaching points
Warming Up	1 Walk in and out of each other.	
	2 Walk along a straight line.	2 *ie.* a floor board or imaginary line.
	3 Run in a straight line, turn on signal, run in another straight line.	
Floor Work	1 Find ways of travelling along a straight line, using your feet in an interesting way.	1 Talk about tight-rope walkers.
	2 Travel along a straight line on your hands and feet.	2 Lines to be kept short.
	3 Find ways of travelling along a straight line using other parts of your body.	

	Content	Teaching points
	4 Make up a phrase by going along a straight line on part of your body, turn and go along another line on a different part.	4 Look at some good examples and discuss why they were good.
Apparatus Activities	1 Use your feet to travel in a straight line along the apparatus.	1 *eg.* along a bench.
	2 Find places where you can climb straight up and down on your apparatus, using your hands and feet.	2 Where possible, *eg.* ropes and climbing frame.
	3 Use other parts of your body to travel along a straight line on your apparatus.	3 Circulate and make suggestions.
	4 Start away from your apparatus on a magic spot. Travel along a straight line up to your apparatus on one part of your body. Move on it how you choose. Travel straight back to your magic spot on another part.	4 Build up gradually Select an example for the class to watch and comment on.
Calming Activity	5 Put the apparatus away.	
	Walk quietly along a straight line.	
	Then: Stand still.	

YEAR 2

Spring Term Session 10: **USING PARTS OF THE BODY**
To travel along a zig-zag pathway

	Content	Teaching points
Warming Up	1 Skip round the rom.	
	2 Hop along a straight line.	2 Real or imaginary.
	3 Do bouncy jumps in and out of each other.	3 Bend knees slightly on take-off and landing.
Floor Work	1 Do bouncy jumps along a zig-zag pathway.	1 Discuss zig-zags first.
	2 Use your hands and feet to travel along a zig-zag pathway.	
	3 Find other parts of your body to travel on, along a zig-zag pathway.	
	4 Make up a phrase of different movements going along a zig-zag pathway.	4 Select one or two examples for the class to watch. Get the children to identify the actions.

	Content	Teaching points
Apparatus Activities	Set it out at angles.	
	1 Find places on your apparatus where you can travel along zig-zag pathways.	1 Circulate and make suggestions.
	2 Use different parts of your body to travel along zig-zag pathways on your apparatus.	
	3 Start away from your apparatus on a magic spot. Travel up to your apparatus on your feet going along a zig-zag pathway. Move on your apparatus anyway you choose. Travel back to your magic spot on your hands and feet.	3 Build up gradually. Select an example for the class to watch and identify the zig-zags.
Calming Activity	Walk quietly round the room. Stand up tall.	

YEAR 2

Spring Term

ASSESSMENT AND CONSOLIDATION SESSION

The children by now should:-

1 Have consolidated all they learnt in the Reception and Year 1.

2 Be able to perform with confidence, control and skill a range of basic actions both on the floor and on the apparatus.

3 Understand and demonstrate that movements can be performed both quickly and slowly, and that varying degrees of strength need to be used in different situations.

4 Be conscious of how the weight of the body can be taken on different parts of the body both in stillness and whilst moving, and transferred from one part to another.

5 Recognize and be able to perform movements in different directions *ie,* forwards, backwards, sideways, up and down.

6 Have begun to use movements in sequence, making up simple phrases of their own, given a basic framework on which to build.

7 Have learnt the correct procedure, established by the school, for lifting, carrying and setting in place the apparatus and mats, putting them away responsibly, (providing the apparatus is suitable for Infants to manage safely).

8 Be aware of what other children are doing in the lesson. Whilst moving they should be conscious of where other children are going and react accordingly.

9 They should be capable of observing other children, commenting constructively on what they see.

10 Be able to demonstrate their movements confidently to the other children and the teacher and discuss their work with competence.

This session can be used to make good any noted weaknesses and repeat any activity which the children found particularly enjoyable.

For your notes and comments.

SPECIFIC SKILLS GUIDE

1 Running

Running is an activity that is seldom taught and which is used mainly for warm-up purposes. Few children, as a result, run well, *ie.* in a mechanically efficient manner.

Children should be taught to bend their arms up, loosely clench their fists, and use a pumping action with their arms to drive the body along. They should bend at the knees and emphasize a high knee lift. They should look where they are going and be taught how to use their feet and twist their shoulders to swerve and dodge in and out of other children when running.

2 Stopping

Children need to be able to stop suddenly. They should be taught to stop with one foot in front of the other, grip tightly with their arm, leg and tummy muscles and bend their knees slightly.

3 Jumping and Landing

Children need to feel the strong thrust upwards through the legs and feet to get height. This can be increased with a vigorous upward swing of the arms.

When jumping off something the children should be taught a 'squashy' landing at first *ie.* bending the knees on impact in a deep squat position. Mats should be used and the children told to land in the middle of the mat and encouraged to land on feet only. The hands may be placed in front of the body after landing if more

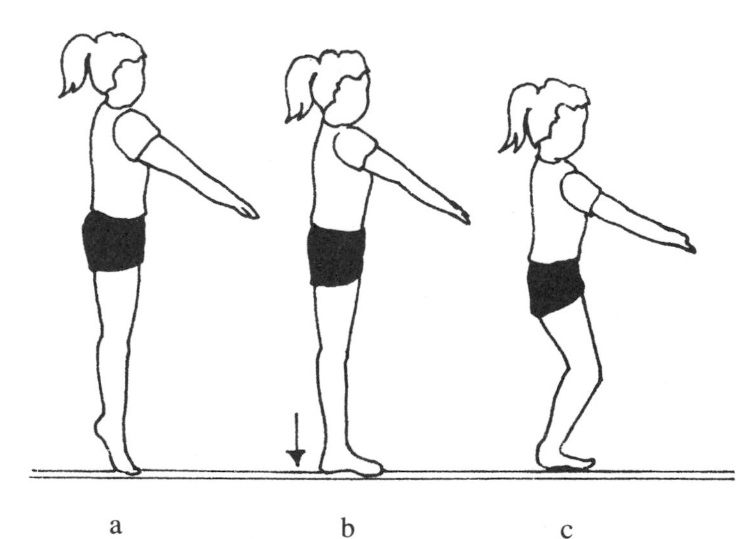

Fig. 1

support is needed at first, but this should be discouraged as soon as is practicable. Children must land on both feet at once.

When jumping on the floor a more resilient landing can be used like a bouncing ball. There is a slight give in the knees on landing and then the body weight is reflected back up again (see *Fig. 1*).

4 Rolling

Mats should be used for rolling actions.

Children should first experience a rolling action by turning the body over sideways – 'rolling like a pencil down a hill'.

They can also roll sideways tucked up 'like a hedgehog', their knees and elbows touching. The hands should not cover the face.

FORWARD ROLLS should not be taught as a class activity until Year 2 by which time the bones in the neck are strong enough. Forward rolls can be taught earlier but only on a one-to-one basis, ensuring the head is safely tucked under.

Children should be shown how to crouch at the end of the mat, feet slightly apart. The hands are placed on the mat and the hips raised. If the knees are parted the children can then be told to look 'backwards, through the window', *ie.* tuck their heads in as closely to the knees as possible. They can then push themselves over onto their backs, reaching forward with their hands to regain standing.

Fig. 2

For further instruction and other ways of rolling see the **Specific Skills Guide** in the second volume *Gymnastics 7-11: A Session-by-Session Approach to Key Stage 2.*

5 Cartwheels

This is a safe activity for children because the weight is being transferred sideways and not forwards as in a handstand. Infants can be taught to do 'mini-cartwheels' as a class activity and proper cartwheels may be attempted by individual children as a result.

Stage 1: Bunny Hops
The hands should be placed flat on the floor in front of the body.
Arms should be straight.
Feet tucked up under the body.
Both feet should come off the floor and land simultaneously.
The children should travel about the room saying 'hands, feet,' to get the correct transference of weight.

Stage 2: Crouch Jumps
As for bunny hops, but on the spot, with emphasis on getting the hips up over the hands.

Children should be shown how to move one hand and shift the weight in the event of the hips passing too far over the line of the inverted body, thus bringing the feet down safely to the starting place.
Care should be taken to ensure the children are spaced out and that there is no likelihood of a child getting kicked.

Stage 3: Starting to Turn
Children can experiment with bringing the feet down to different places on the floor.
By placing the hands slightly to the side of the body and bringing the feet down beyond them the body will have turned through an angle of 180 degrees. The teacher should try to identify those children who turn to the right and who turns to the left.

Stage 4: The Wheeling Action
Talk to the children about wheels and spokes. Explain that the arms and legs are like spokes of a wheel.

Children can try to start the turning action by putting one hand down after the other. Those turning to the right should put the right hand down followed by the left, and vice-versa.

At this stage the legs can remain bent and both feet brought down together.

They can then concentrate on bringing one foot down after the other. It helps if they say, 'foot, hand, hand, foot, foot,' as they move (the first step onto the foot is important for future development of the cartwheel).